# *Conv...*

*by*
**Sylane Mack**

*God's transforming love story
written in my life*

# Convinced!

## by
## Sylane Mack

*God's transforming love story*
*written in my life*

Contact via the ministry Transformed by Grace, Inc.
P.O. Box 976, Newtown, PA 18940 –
Info@transformedbygrace.org
Phone: 215.497.0882 – Website: www.transformedbygrace.org

Published in Association with CreateSpace.com

International Standard Book Number: 144 954 7605
*Printed in the United States of America*

Notes:
1. Chapter 10: "In The Garden," Lyrics written by C. Austin Miles, 1913. Public Domain.
2. Chapter 12: "I Believe in Jesus," Lyrics and Music by Marc Nelson. Copyright © 1987 Mercy/Vineyard Publishing (ASCAP). Administered in North America by Music Services o/b/o Vineyard Music USA. Lyrics reprinted by permission. All rights reserved.

*I dedicate this story of God's transforming love*

*First, to my Jesus – the Author of my salvation,
my healing and my transformation –
only through His love, is this story my truth!
Of this, I am Convinced!*

*and to –*

*My Big Sister, My Oldest Brother,
My Big Brother, My Little Brother,
My Mom and My Dad –
For all that we went through in the dark,
and to celebrate the love of Jesus
that brought us all into His Light!*

**You intended to harm me,
but God intended it for good
to accomplish what is now being done,
the saving of many lives.**
Genesis 50:20

3

# Contents

# *Foreword*

# *God Doesn't Change*

God doesn't change.

I am *convinced* that God is actively, intimately and continually reaching out to all of us. God is reaching out in His passionate, healing love to interrupt and insert Himself into our lives.

No, God doesn't change. *But God has radically changed me.* And God did this with love.

Growing up, I didn't know love. Fleeting moments, yes. But, for the most part, I didn't know love's sweet security. I didn't know its warmth and strength, its tenderness and joy. I didn't know love's encouragement and hope.

Growing up, I mostly knew fear and cruelty, mocking and rejection, anger and hate. I knew much – far too much – of physical, emotional and sexual abuse.

It makes me so sad to know that my story is not that unique. I wish that abuse was not as common as it is. I hate that there is evil in this world. I hate that this evil often comes at us – or is done by us – within the very relationships that should be our safest and sweetest.

There are so many – too many – people who have suffered and may still be suffering to some extent, even years later, because of the cruel hands or the soul-destroying words and actions inflicted on them by another person. There are little ones who are growing up right now and others already grown who are still being hurt and held captive by the destructive power of abuse, neglect and rejection.

But this horrendous hold of victimhood does *not* have to be the end of anyone's story. And as I tell you my story – *God's transforming love story written in my life* – I want you to hear loudly and clearly that I am absolutely, unflinchingly *convinced* that the Lord Jesus Christ, by the power of His love, is able to completely heal, transform and set free the most wounded, broken and imprisoned life.

Jesus did this for me. And God doesn't change. He can do the same for you. Of this, I am *Convinced!*

# 1

## *In the beginning…*
### *Genesis 1:1*

I have no memory of any sexual innocence.

I was somewhere between three and four years old the first time I remember Dad's hands creeping over my body. It must have been during the warmer months (we got a lot of winter months up on Lake Ontario) because I was wearing my favorite nightgown with little pink and orange and blue and purple flowers all over it. And my panties had little flowers on them too, but not as many. I thought I looked so beautiful in this nightie. It was kind of like a Princess dress. I loved to twirl and dance around in my Princess nightie and make it float in the air all around me. I had been doing just that before getting into bed.

The *bed* in our trailer was a bunk bed where three of us kids slept on the bottom bunk and the other two kids slept up on top. There were no assigned places for the five of us kids – two girls and three boys – to sleep. We just got into bed. Always three on the bottom and two on the top.

I wish I had been on the top bunk that night. I wish I had been way up high and all the way back into the farthest corner, pressed against the inside wall of the trailer where Dad couldn't reach me so easily. But on the first night of

*Dad's hands,* I was on the lower bunk and on the very outside edge of the bed.

I had probably hopped into bed last just so I could do *one more* dancing twirl in my beautiful, Princess nightie with all the little flowers. I didn't know my twirl would land me in the danger zone.

I woke up as Dad's hands were pulling my pretty nightie up over my tummy and then rubbing down and all over my panties. I remember his face was so close to mine. But Dad wasn't looking at me. He wasn't seeing me.

But I saw his hands. I saw his hands as they moved from my belly to my bottom. They were so big. With long, black hair on them. The skin on his hands was so much darker than the skin on my little, white belly. His one hand almost covered all of me from the top of my pretty, flowered panties to the top of my ribs. I had never realized before how big his hands were – or how many long, black hairs were on them.

*(There are times, even now – but not as often as when my husband Tim and I were first married – that I have to take my Timmy's hands in mine and really look at them and feel them to reassure myself that these are only the hands of my beautiful husband. These are the hands of my Timmy. And his hands are good. And they are loving. And they will never hurt me.)*

Until that night, I had also never realized how very different Dad's *trigger finger* looked compared to the rest of his fingers. It was a stump, cut off just above his middle knuckle. Dad would tell us kids (and anybody else who was curious enough to ask) in his sing-songy, Mississippi accent how he lost it. *"I wuz jus' fixin' to cut a two-by-four board fo' a goddamned dog house I was buildin', when my* damn kid brother come runnin' over, hollerin' fo' me an' jus' actin' the damn fool. I looked up at the boy, an' shit, if I didn't jus' run the cussed electric saw blade plum through an' cut half my goddamn finger right off. I would'uv whupped the snot right outta the boy right then an' thar if it weren't fo' me needin' to stop the damn blood from runnin' all over hell's creation!" Dad always added a line or two about, "Some gossipin' busy-bodies wuz always sayin' that I'd gone an' chopped off my own goddamn finger cuz I wuz tryin' to get outta the draft or sumthin'. That I know'd they wuzn't never gonna take me into the army without havin' any mo' than a stump fo' a trigger finger on my right hand. Damn fools. They don' know shit. I can still shoot me the eye out-uv-a goddamn diamondback rattlesnake half a mile away." (When this happened Dad was a little over eighteen. It was 1947 – just two years after WWII had ended and right as the Cold War was revving up.)

Dad was in some kind of weird crouching position up near the top corner of the lower bunk, wearing a white, short-sleeved tee shirt with his khaki-colored work pants. He probably had never worn this pair to work, however. They, like his tee shirt, were clean. There were no tell-tale signs from dark grease and tar marks or little burned areas to reveal time spent welding in the trenches of the pipelines.

I stirred and rolled my face sideways on my pillow to look at Dad. His hair (that whenever he got cleaned up, even if he was just heading off to work at some welding site) was always perfectly combed and slicked *just so* with some shiny, sticky stuff to show off his *purdy,* thick, black waves. Those waves were now hanging loose around his face and off to one side. Dad's clean-shaven face was just as tan as his hands and so close to my face that some of his hair was brushing against my forehead and right cheek. But it wasn't a funny-tickling or playful thing where he might have put his hair over my face to make me laugh. I don't think Dad even knew how much of his hair was covering up my face. And it didn't make me laugh.

I could smell and hear his bourbon whiskey breath coming in and out of his mouth and in and out of his long nose as he breathed. He smelled of Old Spice too. I still hate the smell of Old Spice and Aqua Velva. They were Dad's *lying smells*. They were supposed to be nice and smell good to you. But on Dad they just lied and tried to cover up the ugly and the cruel and the evil of him that stunk up my life.

I was so sleepy and so confused. I was so little. All I could get out of my mouth, as I looked back and forth from his face to his big hand covered with long, black hairs and only four and a half fingers, was, *"Daddy?"*

But Dad never looked into my little blue eyes that were the same color as his. He was only looking at my panties.

*"Hush, Laney. You jus' hush up now, y'hear. Jus' you lie still. I'm jus' gonna make you feel good."* And his hand went down under my pretty flowered panties and two of his fingers, not the stump of his trigger finger and not his pinky, went into me.

It didn't feel good.

I sucked in my breath hard and a little high pitched sound came from the top part of my throat. A sound I had never heard coming from me before that night. The sound I would make many more times on many other ugly nights. And the sound that was always the first noise to escape

...right before my screams could finally burst out from deep within me – to shake me awake and shake me out of my terrifying nightmares.

There would be no more noise from me that night. Dad had slapped his other hand tightly over my mouth. It was a big hand too. It covered my face from ear to ear, holding my chin and jaw so tightly that I couldn't open them. His left pinky was pushed up against my little nose. The smell of his Pall Mall cigarettes, that clung to his hand, was jammed up into my nostrils. And Dad's fingers on his right hand kept jamming up inside of me.

It hurt so much. I was so scared. *I didn't even know that I had a hole in my body where his big, hairy fingers could get up inside of me. How did he know? Why was he doing this to me? Why did he wake me up? Why didn't he look at me? Where was Mom? Where was our little fox terrier, Tanya, who always slept under the bottom bunk of our bed? Was she scared too? I knew Tanya wouldn't bite Dad. She was a good dog. But I wanted her to bite him now. I wanted her to make him stop. She must have been put outside. She was probably running around in the woods or playing down at the river. I wished I was outside in the woods or down at the river. I wished I was with Tanya.*

I wiggled and squirmed and tried to push Dad's hands away from my mouth and out of my bottom. He held my jaw tighter and pushed his fingers harder and faster. I wanted to throw up. I was sick and dizzy. My stomach hurt so much. My bottom and the hole I didn't even know I had hurt so much. I wanted to be invisible. I think I was to him. He never looked into my eyes. *Daddy! Daddy, what are you doing? Why are you hurting me? Why did you lie to*

*me? This doesn't feel good. I'm so sick. You're so mean. I
hate you! Stop it! Stop it! Stop it!*

For a moment Dad stopped touching my hole with his right hand, but his left hand still squeezed my mouth shut. He unbuttoned his pants, unzipped them and folded the front panels back so that they made a V on his hips. He reached through and unsnapped the black and gray zig-zaggy patterned boxer shorts he was wearing. He pulled out his *tee-tee thing.* I had seen it before.

The trailer that we five kids, Mom and Dad lived in was tight quarters with one bathroom. And that bathroom was actually part of the hallway which ran from the back of the trailer where my parents' room was, continued through the bathroom, then through our kids' room – actually dividing those three rooms in half, with closets on one side of the hallway and my parents' bed, bathroom sink, toilet, tub and our kids' bunk bed on the other – and finally opened up into our kitchen-dining-living room area. In such a small living-and-lack-of-privacy space with two adults and five children (all born within fewer than five years of each other), there was almost always somebody going pee in our hallway bathroom. So I had seen Dad's *tee-tee thing* before.

But now Dad reached for it and it was different. It was scary. He gripped it hard and it grew even bigger and fatter and longer. *What was happening to him? What was he doing to me?* My pretty, flowered panties were hanging down somewhere between my knee and my left ankle. I tried to pull them back on and push him away from me.

Dad took his hand off my mouth just long enough to pull my beautiful, Princess nightie up over my head. He slammed his hand back hard across my mouth again, even before my nightie had the chance to settle its pretty, air-floating flowers all the way down onto my pillow.

As he held and squeezed his *tee-tee thing,* I was just glad his fingers had stopped pushing into my hole. But, then, Dad pulled me up, put his knees against the bed and sat me down hard onto his *tee-tee thing...*turned monster and devil and killer. My pretty flowered panties fell off my ankle onto the yellow, speckled linoleum floor. And the hole that I didn't even know I had, was viciously invaded and attacked. And I hated Dad. And I wanted to die.

*How could the others sleep? Or were they awake? But maybe they were really scared too? Where Was My Mom?*

*No. This couldn't be.* I could now move my eyes all the way to the right where the hallway entered into the bathroom. Mom was standing back just a bit from the door frame. She was just standing there, leaning against the bathroom closet door with her arms folded in front of her just under her chest. She was wearing her gray, knit pants and a red, lightweight sweatshirt. She looked so relaxed. Every once in awhile a little bit of light coming in from Mom and Dad's room would reflect off her glasses. And Mom just stood there and watched. She just watched. She just watched. *Mom? Mom!* She never looked into my eyes either.

Dad kept shoving and pushing me. Hurting me. Killing me. It looked like it was hurting him too. His face, which was usually very handsome, was ugly, all squished together and frighteningly distorted. He didn't even look like Dad. His blue eyes were hidden behind his eyelids that were shut more firmly, and with more wrinkles, than I had ever seen them before. It didn't matter. He wasn't using his eyes to see me. Dad was only using his hands and his *tee-tee thing.*

One hand to keep my mouth slammed shut, the other to keep plunging me on his *tee-tee thing* which was ripping my insides out of me. Loud snorts were coming out his long nose, his nostrils flaring wildly to the rhythm of his snorts and pushes. My throat kept trying to make noises, trying to scream from as deep within me as Dad was plunging.

Dad's hands on me were all sweaty now. Drips came from under his chin and dribbled down onto his white, now sweat-soaked, tee shirt. Dad suddenly clinched his jaw shut with an ugly ferocity and jerked his neck and head back hard. I thought his Adam's apple was going to come flying out of his throat like a rocket. But the explosion wasn't from his throat. An evil, enemy's bomb had exploded up inside of me, inside of my hole that I didn't even know I had. I was sure that the heat pummeling from Dad's *tee-tee thing* was going to burn me to death from the inside out. *I would melt away like the wicked witch from the <u>Wizard of Oz</u>. But I wasn't wicked! I was good! This shouldn't be happening to me!*

I felt a sickening pull from the deepest part of my body as Dad suddenly dropped to his knees onto the yellow, speckled linoleum floor. He was panting hard and fast like Tanya sometimes did after she ran a long way on a scorching summer day. His right knee landed on top of my pretty flowered panties. I wanted them back. His *tee-tee thing* was dribbling goo onto the floor. *It* was changing back to how I had seen it before. Dad still held my mouth with his left hand, but, because his hand was shaking a bit, his grip was a little looser and didn't squeeze my face so tightly anymore. His right hand was holding onto my left thigh and bottom. It was shaking too. My hole oozed messy, stinky stuff onto the edge of the bed.

Down on his knees, Dad lifted his drooped and panting head and *finally* looked into my eyes. His grip on my mouth now turned into just his pointer finger pressing hard against my lips. My little mouth, partially freed, was now squished up into a pout and starting to shake out of control. I started to cry. I started to talk. I had so much I wanted to say. So much I wanted to ask him. But his finger's press against my lips got firmer. *"Now, hush, Laney. You jus' hush up. Don' you dare wake up those other kids. You jus' hush up. Don' you dare say one word. Not one goddamn word. You jus' hush up now. Git yourself dried off an' then git your droopy drawers back into bed. An' I don' wanna hear not one goddamn peep outta you, y'hear?"* I just nodded.

Dad repeated, *"Y'hear me now, Laney?"* He took a firm hold of my chin, his now-cruel, blue eyes were not only looking at me, they were boring into me, almost as hard as his *tee-tee thing* had. Jerking his renewed grip on my face, Dad forced my blue eyes to meet his. *"Y'hear me now, Laney? Not one goddamn peep outta you, or I'll give you a whuppin' that you'll never forget."* He gave my chin one more hard, rough squeeze. I could barely squeak out of my trembling, squished-together mouth the required, *"Yessir."*

When I did, Dad was satisfied. He pushed himself up off from his knees and onto his feet. He shot a quick look over at the other two sleeping children who shared the lower bunk with me that night and who had wiggled themselves closer to the trailer wall, away from the danger zone. Dad also glanced up into the top bunk to check on the two sleeping there. Then he entered the bathroom. I watched

Mom hand him an old white towel just before she closed the door behind him. *I hate her. I hate Dad.*

The water in the sink ran for awhile as they spoke in low voices. I couldn't understand their words. I couldn't understand anything. I just sat there shaking, tears were dripping down. But I didn't make *one goddamn peep*.

The toilet flushed. The light in the bathroom went out. I heard the back door of the trailer open from my parents' bedroom. Tanya came scooting into the hallway like nothing had happened. She was heading straight for her sleeping spot under the lower bunk. But she stopped and put her nose to work sniffing my pretty, flowered panties that were still on the floor. I slipped down from the edge of the bed, grabbing my not-so-Princess-nightie off my pillow, and got the gooey, sticky, stinky stuff all over my legs and backside before my feet hit the floor. I took my panties away from Tanya's nose. She looked at me, tilting her head to one side. I think she was confused too.

I went pee. It took about a half roll of toilet paper to wipe me dry from all the goo and the blood – which I just noticed for the first time under the bright bathroom light. I got a wash cloth out of the closet, wetting it with water from the tub's faucet. I tried to get all the yuck out of me and off of me. But I kept very quiet, at least until I threw up. And even then I tried to be quiet.

I pulled the little stool in place so I would be tall enough to reach up high to get a drink of water from the sink. My mouth tasted really bad from the throw-up. I rinsed and spit, then climbed onto the edge of our yellow tub to watch my spit go swirling down the drain. It also was tinged with a little bit of blood. I must have bitten the inside of my cheek when Dad was squeezing my mouth so hard.

*(Even now, I still shudder just a little bit whenever anyone goes to grab my mouth or squeeze my face, even if they're just being funny. It's not funny to me.)*

My vomity-bloody spit went swirling down the drain, and it was never going to come back to our sink. I wanted to swirl away with it. *Did it come up anywhere?* I peeked into the bathroom mirror. Normally, I would have smiled at myself. I liked my curly, blond-light-brown hair (which is now straight and dark). I liked my blue eyes. But tonight my face was still marked with red and white coloring that traced out Dad's left hand. And my eyes looked different. They were darker. I didn't smile at myself in the mirror. I didn't know how.

I pulled my panties back in place making sure they weren't inside out. I hugged my favorite flowered Princess nightie to my chest before tugging it over my head. Tanya was still right where I left her when I went into the bathroom. She stayed awake and was waiting for me. I think Tanya wanted to make sure I was all right.

I didn't hop back into bed. I couldn't. I didn't ever want to be in that bad place again. I felt my mouth start to quiver as it shaped itself into that tight, little pout circle again. The tears started dropping. I pulled my pillow down from the ugly bed and crawled underneath the bottom bunk to sleep with Tanya. I was shaking and scared. And so sick to my stomach.

But neither of us made *one goddamn peep.*

# 2

## *And there was evening and there was morning...*
### *Genesis 1:5*

Feet, lots of them – some bare, some with socks on – walked past my sleeping spot with Tanya.

The bottom bunk was pretty high off the ground. So underneath it, as long as I positioned myself just right in between the lengths of raw, wooden two-by-fours used to support the bottom bunk, I was still small enough to sit up straight without ever bumping my head. It was a good place to hide and be quiet.

Besides being the place where Tanya slept, this good hiding place was used as a keeping place for extra stuff like blankets, a few toys and clothing that would eventually be passed down between us five kids until a particular item was deemed either too small or too worn out to be kept any longer. One reason I loved my beautiful, Princess nightie with the little pink and orange, blue and purple flowers all over it so much was because it had *always and only been mine*. And I was the youngest girl in the family, so it would never belong to anyone else. Never. Only to me.

I still had not made *one goddamn peep* as I watched the march of feet go by back and forth down the trailer hallway. Then, the feet with the dark socks and gray work pants stopped. One knee went down to the floor and Dad's big, smiling face and light blue eyes peered at me underneath the bottom bunk.

*"Laney! Girl, what in tar-nation are you doin' underneath that bed? Aren't you afraid that the Boogey-Man might git up after you! Come on outta thar right now, y'here! An' git your droopy drawers right up to that breakfast table."*

When Dad's face appeared my stomach fell. I was confused and sick. I was afraid I was going to throw up all over again. But I didn't make a move to come out from under that bed. *He's the one I'm afraid of! NOT the Boogey-Man! I don't want Dad here! I don't want to see him! I don't want to hear him! I don't want him to touch me! He's mean! He hurts me! I hate him! Go away! Leave me alone! You're bad! I hate you!* But I still didn't make *one goddamn peep.*

I just scooted back a little bit further underneath the bottom bunk, but a box of something stopped me from pushing myself any closer to the back wall of the trailer. I pulled my Princess nightie over my legs as far down as it would go, and then, I pulled Tanya up onto my lap. I felt just a little safer that way. Tanya was a little too big to really fit on my lap, even though she was a small fox terrier. Her front paws and face went beyond my left leg, her tail and back paws were touching the floor on my right side. As I pulled her into place, Tanya licked my cheek and nose. She really was such a good dog.

*"Laney! You come on outta thar, right now! Day's a-wasting!"* Dad's voice was almost laughing, like he thought it was funny and cute that I would be hiding underneath the bed with Tanya. There was no trace of

anger in his southern sing-songy voice. I still didn't make a move except to pull Tanya in just a little tighter to me. Dad walked into the kitchen saying something, still with a bit of a laugh in his voice, about *"...that damn-fool girl sleepin' down thar with that damn-fool dog..."*

Then, other feet and their attached faces appeared with different words and different reactions to my hideout. My three brothers – two bigger than me, one smaller – in various stages of dress, but all in white tee shirts, peeked their heads, one at a time, underneath the bottom bunk.

My (one year older than I am and a lot bigger) Big Brother pretty much ignored me. His round, blue eyes never really looked at me. He just looked at Tanya. He slapped both his legs with his palms, calling for Tanya to come out and play with him. She did. Tanya just sped off my lap and, with her tail wagging and feet jumping excitedly all over My Big Brother, she went right out to play with him. Tanya never even looked back to make sure I was okay. I pulled my Princess nightie back over my legs. She had kicked it up over my knees in her big hurry to leave me so she could go play with My Big Brother. Neither Tanya nor My Big Brother saw my sad little face, lips pushed down and together and shaking just a little bit, when they left me. They weren't looking at me.

That was how much of my relationship with My Big Brother seemed to be throughout most of our childhood. I was *not ever really seen by him* – not for me. Not as a real, (lovable, singing, dancing, playful, smart) whole person. I mostly felt ignored by him, which in my family was definitely a good deal better than being brutalized. But Dad's evil, narcissistic teaching, which victimized, coerced and opened twisted doors of sexuality between all of us children – and Mom's silent approval which allowed for it all – brought, even between My Big Brother and me, the bizarre sickness of incest that played out in our early years. That My Big Brother even brought some of his friends into, and into me.

During those times, I would be *seen by him*, at least momentarily, and then ignored again. Unless I could bring some benefit to him. I was seen whenever he wanted me to connect him up with one of my girlfriends. I was seen when I was needed to type his high school term papers. It seemed that he and Mom and Dad actually *expected* this from me. After all, I had been *uppity* enough to want an electric typewriter for my own school work. I should help him out. It was only right.

The other times I would be *seen by him* usually seemed to be when I was *seen as an embarrassment to him*.

One day as a first-grader, I had the audacity to wear my favorite, pink-fluffy Bunny slippers to school. (I had cleverly *hidden* my real shoes under my bed so that I would *have to* wear my only alternative: my pink-fluffy Bunny slippers.) My Big Brother, an older, wiser and a-heck-of-a-lot-bigger-than-me second-grader, was completely outraged to see me enter the school cafeteria wearing my pink-fluffy Bunny slippers. He yelled at me in front of everybody, shaking his finger and pointing to the door, *"Go home! Get those stupid bunny slippers off your feet and put your real shoes on! I can't believe you're wearing those to school! You're so stupid! I am not your brother!"* Well, apparently my sense of fashion and fun just didn't appeal to him. I shrank at his anger and at the intensity of the embarrassment I had caused him because others knew that I was, indeed, his *stupid* little sister.

At that time, and only while I was in first and second grade, we lived in the inner city of East Hartford, Connecticut, where we walked to and from Silver Lane Elementary School. (All the rest of my growing up years, from right around age three until seventeen, was spent in a very small, rural town near Lake Ontario in central New York.) So, because I *could* in East Hartford, I *did* what My *embarrassed* Big Brother told me to do. I walked home.

I left school, walked down the street crying my eyes out and dragging my little Bunny-slippered feet the entire four or five blocks back to the one half, old duplex house my family rented during our two year stint in CT. I quickly *found* my real shoes under my bed and explained to Mom what had happened. She just laughed at me, but not meanly. Which was good. I was so upset and felt so stupid.

Later she laughed again when My Big Brother told Mom *his version* of the tale of my *lost shoes* and my *stupid Bunny slippers*. They laughed about this particular story many times. And over the years, they found a whole repertoire of stories to laugh about because of my embarrassing, and often, klutzy-clumsy ways.

But now, being appropriately dressed in *my real shoes*, I just walked right back to Silver Lane Elementary School, all by myself, just as I would have done if I had planned to walk home during my lunch period (which was strangely allowed by the school district – and which gave greater wings to my already growing, fiercely independent streak). I never did eat lunch that day, even though Mom offered to make me something. I just didn't feel much like eating. Feeling stupid has a way of shutting down my appetite. Even now.

Other times when I was seen as an embarrassment to My Big Brother were because I just wasn't *cool enough* for him. This was true. He was really popular and very cute. He was funny and easily the center of attention with everyone. I was not.

And when God *really* turned my life around in my early teens and called me to passionately live out my faith in Him both in my home and at school – I was definitely *not cool*. (I'll be the first to admit that my adolescent passion for Jesus was powerful, aka obnoxious and overwhelming, at times. I have since learned greater patience, gentleness and the *wisdom of silence* as evidenced by the deep scars on my tongue from biting it so hard and so often that blood would dribble down my cheeks.)

So, I was not only an embarrassment to My Big Brother, *but now*, because of my living-it-out-loud-faith, I was also someone or something to be absolutely avoided.

Even so, during our teen years, My Big Brother and I had some deep, spiritual talks once I began to openly live out my relationship with Jesus *and* after the incest between us had stopped. *(We both, very early on, directed our energies to getting and staying away from the sickness of our home as much as possible. Sports, clubs, all kinds of school activities and friends legitimately limited our time at home. I believe, too, that there was a very real and righteous, protective shame inflicted by God's judgment against incest that kept him and his friends away from me.)*

And as strange as it sounds – *because God's grace and truth still speak in the darkest of places* – there would be those sweet and unexpected times when My Big Brother and I would have those really deep, spiritual talks about Jesus, about His salvation, about His forgiveness. Our talks weren't all that frequent. And they were almost always initiated (and pushed on him) by me – *the Jesus freak.*

Still, our talks were special and meaningful even if hard and awkward for both of us. When the rush of being cool, funny and popular momentarily slowed down around him, I could clearly see what I always knew was there – a very real softness and sensitivity in My Big Brother's heart towards others. And there was almost always a softness in him towards God.

But for so many years, My Big Brother had learned to be cool. Avoid the pain. Deny the ugly. Have fun. Be the Fun One in the crowd. Keep the people laughing. *It's not really all that bad. Don't think about it. Keep going. Have fun. It'll all work out.*

It was easier for My Big Brother to just keep on going, laugh and make others laugh rather than face the ugly reality of a family deeply entrenched in such cruel abuse and sick incest. This created a gap in our relationship that waxed and waned over the years – and always made me sad during our more distant times. But I just couldn't laugh off the ugly. Ugly evil isn't funny.

Mom and Dad had shriveled and clouded up in me, in every one of us five kids – and in themselves – any possibility of knowing what *true love* and *true intimacy* really are. *Love* in its most basic form is unselfish and sacrificial. *Intimacy* in its most basic form is complete trust and willing vulnerability. Instead, we were all – at some level and in far too many ways – learning and growing in selfishness, self-delusions, self-pity, self-destruction and self-protection.

*I thank God that this is not where He left us.*

But *that morning*, after Dad's first rape of me, I was holding tightly onto a small piece of the ruffled hem on my beautiful, flowered, Princess nightie. My pouty little face still quivering. My Big Brother had never really looked at me. He had not really seen me. I watched him run off to play with Tanya. They would both have more fun with each other. More fun than they would have hanging out with me underneath the bottom bunk. *Would I ever have fun again? Would I ever want to play again? Would My Big Brother ever look me in my eyes and care about me? Does Tanya love him more than she loves me? I was pretty sure Mom loved him more than me. She shouldn't have. But she did. I didn't blame him. That was how Mom was.*

I lifted my Princess nightie hem up just a little bit as I folded myself over to meet it on my way down. Its little, puffed, flowery sleeves weren't big enough or long enough to reach my face. I needed to wipe my runny nose and dry my cheeks from the tears that had just started rolling over them again.

My tears were almost dry when My (two years older than I am) Oldest Brother's feet came into view at the edge of the bed. He had big, wide toes, bare, thick legs and was wearing gray and red plaid shorts. I pulled my Princess nightie back down, bent my legs at the knees, quickly tucked my feet up under my nightie and held my legs together tightly with my shaking and tired little hands.

*I wished I was invisible.*

My Oldest Brother looked at me underneath the bottom bunk with his big, wide face and just kind of glared at me. His blue eyes were a near-translucent, steely blue (and almost always a little scary to me). They were encircled by a very dark outer rim. His eyes almost jumped out at me, appearing bluer and more piercing because of his darker coloring – both of hair and skin. As he stared at me in my hiding place, the right corner of his mouth went up into a condemning, half-smirk. He shook his head and just said, with a tightness in his jaw and voice, *"You're so stupid. You're not hiding from anybody under there!"*

My Oldest Brother was almost always meaner to me than my other siblings. At least in the very obvious ways. It seemed like he was almost always angry. At everything. At everyone. And he was always the most dangerous and violent towards me as we grew up. He had learned far too well from our Dad's abusive cruelty. My Oldest Brother had suffered horrendously – both sexually and from the violent beatings that Dad inflicted on us.

The poison infecting my family was clearly evident in My Oldest Brother's behavior. As he grew, he became so obviously sick and twisted by the hands and hurts of Dad. He was so aggressive and always sexually taunting and terrorizing. His taunting would flow constantly from his *dirty, swear-word-infested* mouth. He would frequently go from accusing me of being *"a slut"* in one moment (and well before I even knew *what* that word meant) to ridiculing me in the next moment for being *"a carpenter's dream, because you're as flat as a board and never been nailed."* (And *this* came well after *that* was no longer true in my life – at least the part about never being nailed.)

My Oldest Brother terrorized me by following Dad's flagrant example and habits of exhibitionism and violent masturbation. He often hid in the lowest part of the bathroom closet (which had to be *open in* the bathroom in order to *close off* the bathroom from the hallway) down under some dirty clothes so he could watch me in the tub.

Too many times, when I realized he was there, he would start grabbing at me, touching me, rubbing me, raping me. He was always overpowering, always controlling. His steely blue eyes always hating me. And a sickness and a sick smile and a sick laugh oozed from him and killed me more and more and more. *Why did he do this to me? Why did no one ever come to stop this? Why did no one hear me screaming for help when My Oldest Brother attacked me? Why did they allow this to happen to me over and over again? I hate my family! They must hate me.*

In the bathroom I was always vulnerable. But no place was truly safe for me. My Oldest Brother would chase me down – both inside the trailer and outside in the fields or back in the woods or down at the river – forcing himself on me and in me so many times throughout our childhood. Just like Dad. There was no safe place to hide from him or from Dad. Nowhere. No matter how hard I tried. No matter where I hid.

When we moved back from Connecticut to our New York property, Dad built a new section onto our trailer. We had all grown and needed more space. This bigger, better trailer make-over – known as *the addition* – included a living room, a laundry entry/exit room and, eventually, two other pass-through bedrooms with deep-shelved closets. One of those closet shelves became, for a little bit of time anyway, a safe zone for me. I hid in that closet, curling myself up into the tightest ball I could force my body into, breathing as quietly as possible. I would stay in that position. In the dark. For hours. (This has become a bit of a BLURSE – this is my own special word that means: *The combination of a Blessing and a Curse.* It's a BLURSE for me because, for a woman who now carries an AARP card, I am outrageously, incredibly flexible – *Blessing*. But this blessing came from spending all those terrified hours hiding in the corner of that closet shelf, curled into that outrageously, contortionistic position – *Curse*. BLURSE.)

I hid so that I would not be found. Not by My Dad, not by My Oldest Brother. I didn't want anyone to find me. I didn't want anyone to touch me or hurt me. Ever again.

But just like he did on *that morning* after Dad's first rape of me, when he found me underneath the bottom bunk, My Oldest Brother found me years later in my hiding spot – curled up in the corner of that closet shelf. He was older, stronger, bigger, his eyes even steelier and more hate-filled, his voice even more menacing. But his words were almost identical, *"You're so stupid. You're not hiding from anybody up here!"* His rough, wide hands grabbed at me, ripping me out from the closet shelf...ripping me out from my hiding spot, and then he ripped into my body, once more. Cruelly. Mockingly. Violently.

*I just died inside my head. While my body was being used. I was not there. I was not a person. I had no person. I had no safety. I had no closet to crawl into anymore. I just crawled deeper and deeper inside my head. Into numbness. Into nothingness.*

When this sick abuse began, My Oldest Brother was just a little child too. Just like the rest of us. He wasn't supposed to become so sick and twisted. None of us were. It was caused by the ugly and the evil that was allowed by Mom and Dad – and modeled and taught in our home. *This wasn't right. Not for me! Not for him! Not for any of us! Where was the safety that a home and family should be? Where were the expressions and lessons of love and kindness, purity and innocence? Why was there already so*

*much ugly and hate, evil, meanness and hurt in my family?*
*Why did we all have so much poison killing each of us in*
*our own ways? Why did I always have to look for a place to*
*hide? Why was there no safe place to hide?*

Two more feet stopped right at the edge of the bottom
bunk – and almost a whole body. These feet had little pink
toes and belonged to My Little Brother (one year younger
than I, two years behind me in school). Back then, at
around two and a half years old, he really was My *Little*
Brother, and at that time he was a good deal shorter than I
was. (Not anymore! He's now over six feet tall, while I
personally topped off at the grand height of five feet, two
inches.)

My Little Brother was skinny and cute. He was a
*towhead,* with blond hair, pale skin and big question marks
in his light blue, little boy eyes. He was often sickly with
asthma – maybe caused in part by Mom and Dad's heavy,
chain-smoking of cigarettes in the very tight quarters of our
trailer. (The Surgeon General hadn't yet gotten around to
telling the world of the dangers of second-hand smoke.) My
Little Brother had to sleep from time to time on the bottom
bunk under an oxygen tent during his early childhood
years. That morning he scooted himself into my hiding
place and right up beside me, *"Wanna play, Laney?"*

We often pretended lots of different, happy things
together when we were little. Just a few years later when
the TV show *Bewitched!* became one of our favorite shows
*ever*, My Little Brother and I would spend hours running
around outside, wiggling our noses and making all kinds of
fun and magic things happen in our lives. Pretending with
My Little Brother was one tiny, sweet hold of childlike
innocence that I had left to me.

Some time about two years later, when I was once again in the danger zone on the bottom bunk, with My Little Brother sleeping next to me that night, Dad stole the innocent relationship from the two of us who were known as *The Babies* of the family. With Mom at her watching post – part in shadow, part in light – resting up against the frame of the bathroom doorway, Dad woke me up just as he was taking My Little Brother's hand to touch me on my bottom, and my hand to touch him. *Why!!?? Why do you steal and kill and destroy everything? Dad! Mom! Why do you ruin everything? Why do you hate us? Why is there nothing left to us? I hate you both so much! I hate you both!*

Still, My Little Brother and I had some pretending left in us. Mostly to pretend that this kind of thing didn't happen.

Later in high school, when I was a senior and My Little Brother (who was now My-*not-so*-Little-Brother-*anymore*) was a sophomore, we got to put our well-rehearsed acting talents to the test in front of an audience as we sang, danced and spoke in two of the lead roles for the play *Godspell*.

It was all that much more meaningful to me because by then I was living out, actively and openly, my faith in Jesus as my Savior and Lord. For me, this play was one way I could declare publicly that Jesus Christ is the Son of God, the Savior of the world. I even talked (Okay! I *harassed and begged!)* our fabulous Teaching Staff, aka Senior Play Directors, into changing the last scene of *Godspell* from how it was originally written so that our version would make it absolutely clear that Jesus rose from the dead! This was a non-negotiable for me. There was no pretending about that for me! None at all.

But *that morning* when My Little Brother crawled underneath the bottom bunk and asked me, *"Wanna play, Laney?"* I didn't really feel like playing. Not with him. Not with anybody. I was glad for his company, though, and for his smiling little face that wanted me to spend time with him. But I just couldn't. Not then. I looked down at my lap where Tanya had been protecting me just moments before, and where Dad had hurt me so badly just hours before. I just shook my head, *No*. Still without making *one goddamn peep.*

My Little Brother grabbed a little truck from the toys stuffed underneath the bottom bunk and just scooted himself right back out. He was making happy *vrrroooomm-vrrroooomm* noises as he pushed his little red truck down the yellow linoleum hallway of our trailer.

Then came another pair of feet, attached to legs much longer and leaner than mine. My Big Sister! Oh! I loved her so much! She was so nice and so pretty. Dad called her *Princess*. Her sparkly, blue eyes were so light, and so was her skin. She had bouncy, beautiful hair and a big, wide smile and a big laugh – whenever she did laugh. But *that morning*, she didn't give me her big smile or her big laugh as she peeked underneath the bottom bunk. But she gave me kindness and a gentle smile. *"Laney-Lou..." (Only she ever called me Laney-Lou, which ended up morphing into Louie for awhile during our high school years. And which, again, only she ever called me. My Big Sister even wrote out part of her message to me on the back of her beautiful, senior picture by addressing me as Louie. I loved that. But only from her.)*

Bent from her waist, My Big Sister softly spoke in her kind, older sister tone, *"Laney-Lou, come on out from underneath there now. It's time to get dressed, eat some breakfast and get on with the day."* She really was *The Big Sister*. The first born. And she seemed so grown up to me right then. She was somewhere between seven and eight years old herself.

My Big Sister was almost always nice to me. We didn't play a lot together as young children. There's a three years and (a little over) eight months difference in our ages. And when you're a little kid that is a *very big* difference for how you like to spend your time. I was a tomboy and loved to play outside and climb trees, hike in the woods, play at the river, ride my bike and run fast. Very fast. (I was once nicknamed *Lightning*. Oh! Those days have *long* since passed!) My Big Sister always seemed so mature and happy to be quieter. She was really smart and did very well in school. She read a lot.

The older she got, and especially after we moved back to New York following our two year stint in Connecticut (the fall she entered sixth grade and I entered third), we still didn't *play* a lot together, but we would *do* more things together. Sometimes in the middle of the night, My Big Sister would wake me up and ask me if I wanted to be a *Brownie Elf* with her. (We had both joined the Girl Scouts while in Connecticut. Our small, rural hometown in NY didn't have a Girl Scout chapter. It still doesn't.) As *Elves* we would sneak quietly out of bed to secretly help by cleaning up around the trailer – leaving little notes that said, *"Cleaned by the Elves!"* or *"The Elves were here!"* I loved being an *Elf* with My Big Sister.

By the time I was in sixth grade, it seemed that our chronological age difference didn't make so much of a difference anymore. I was *so old* for my age on so many levels by then. (Even starting my period at age ten when I started sixth grade.) And My Big Sister seemed to recognize my maturity by *doing* a few more things with me. Sometimes with some of her bigger friends or sometimes with just the two of us, we would take the bus all the way from our little town to go into the big city of Syracuse to go shopping *downtown*. This made me love her even more. Not many big sisters were *this kind* to their little sisters. I was so proud that she would invite me to do such a grown-up thing with her, especially when she went with her friends. I would do anything for My Big Sister. And I always tried to be on my very best – and very coolest – behavior around her cool, older friends.

My Big Sister seemed to become more and more popular, both with her peers and her teachers, with each passing year. She always seemed to have lots of friends, and her big laugh seemed to come more and more often. She was involved in all kinds of school activities – and a leader in just about every way possible – from Student Council, to International Club, to Princess of her Junior Prom, to Co-editor of her Senior Class Year Book. She was cool, fun, smart and popular. I was so proud of her.

All these activities helped My Big Sister to stay away from home as much as possible. Which meant she was staying away from me too.

But in our home, there was never really a way to stay completely away from the ugly, the sick and the evil. Not in the middle of the night. Not in the middle of the day when there was no school. I know. I tried to stay away from home as much as possible, too, as I got older and could be busy with friends and school activities. This never worked. At least never well enough.

And my disappearing underneath the bottom bunk after Dad's meanness and hurting of me so badly just the night before, didn't keep me hidden, or away, either.

While My Big Sister was still looking at me, I saw the ankle-high, white socks on Mom's feet walk by without a pause in her pace. Mom was wearing the same gray, knit pants from the night before. But I couldn't see if she had on the same red, light-weight sweatshirt. Mom never stopped by the edge of the bed. She never bent down. Mom never looked at me underneath the bottom bunk. Mom never fixed it. *Moms are supposed to fix all hurts. Moms are not supposed to watch the hurts and let them happen.*

My Big Sister's voice came again, *"Laney-Lou, come on out. It's okay."*

But in my head – in my little head that just wanted to put on some funny hat and dance and twirl around again in my beautiful, Princess nightie with the little pink and orange and blue and purple flowers all over it – I knew My Big Sister was wrong. It wasn't okay.

It was very much *not* okay.

# 3

## ...Sin is crouching at your door; it desires to have you...
*Genesis 4:7*

Mom never looked at me. She never came to make sure *I* was okay. She walked by my hiding place. Her ankle-high, white socks and her gray, knit pants just walked by. She had other more important things to do.

Mom called everybody to breakfast. I didn't want to go. I didn't want to sit with everybody. I wanted to throw up. I wanted to disappear forever.

I knew I had to go to breakfast. I knew I had to act like I was okay. I knew I was not to say one word or ask anyone anything about what Dad had done to me and what Mom had watched. I knew I was never supposed to make *one goddamn peep* about it.

But my mind was making a lot more than just a few *goddamn peeps*. My mind was shouting at me. But my mouth didn't open. My head was hurting as it spun around and around trying to put into words what I wasn't supposed to say aloud.

*I wish Tanya were here with me right now. I think I would feel stronger. I feel so weak. I feel so weird. I am different. Everything is different. I feel so alone. How could that be when everybody's here? When seven of us live in this trailer? How could Mom have watched all the bad stuff that Dad did to me and not stop it? Aren't we supposed to be nice and help people when we see them getting hurt? Why did Dad do this bad stuff to me? Why did he hurt my body so that it will never ever be the same again? Does he hate me? Does Mom hate me? I hate them. But they're My Mom and Dad! They're supposed to love me! I'm supposed to love them! Why don't they love me? What did I do wrong? I didn't do anything wrong! But they're big. They know things I don't. They're supposed to take care of me. They're My Mom and Dad! I am so mad at them! I am so confused. So scared. So sore.*

*And I have to be so silent!*

I rubbed my bottom and noticed how yucky my beautiful, Princess nightie felt where I had been sitting. The mean, oozing, sticky stuff from Dad (that I thought I had washed all off of me and all out of my hole that I didn't know I had) must have dried into this crusty, crunchy, weird layer.

*I hate them so much! My beautiful, Princess nightie wasn't beautiful anymore. I wasn't beautiful anymore.* I wasn't an innocent, little girl anymore. *I wasn't anything.*

*Maybe I never was.*

I crawled out from underneath the bottom bunk. I stood up and looked down at my little bare feet. They weren't twirling me around anymore. I think they forgot how.

Mom called us all to breakfast again. Without a twirl, without anything – except a sick feeling way down deep in my deepest belly – I grabbed a pair of red shorts, a yellow tee shirt and some different panties. I went into the bathroom shutting both doors. Pulling my nightie off over my head, I didn't hug it to myself this time. It was ugly and crusty and ruined. That's how I felt too. I tried not to even look at it as I threw it into the dirty clothes basket inside the bathroom closet. I took off my panties quickly and pulled on my clean ones even quicker. And even quicker than that, I pulled on my shorts and tee shirt.

*I don't ever want to be naked again.*

Now it was Dad's voice, "*Laney, git your butt up to this here table! Right now! Didn't you hear your mother callin' you! You think you're as good as a white girl! Makin' us all wait on you!*"

I opened the back door to the bathroom first. It was just a few steps away from the door leading out of the trailer. I wanted to run. I wanted to leave. *But this is my home! This is my family!* I heard everybody's voices in the kitchen and the chairs moving against the yellow linoleum as my family took their seats around the table. I heard My Two Older Brothers banging into each other a bit.

Dad's voice was a little louder, a little meaner, "*Laney, goddamn it! Git outta that bathroom and do as you're told!*"

I did as I was told. I opened the door between the bathroom and the rest of the trailer – the hallway seemed longer, the kitchen farther away. And it seemed like everyone except Mom, whose back faced me, was watching me as I entered the kitchen. I got up into the seat in between My Big Sister and My Little Brother. My Oldest Brother and My Big Brother were sitting on the opposite side of the table. With Mom and Dad at the ends. White, pink, green, yellow and blue – very durable (very often used over the years) and almost translucent – plastic cups stood guard at the border of each of our children's breakfast plates. Mom and Dad had coffee cups, and ever-present ashtrays, at theirs.

Then, as bizarre and incongruous as I felt, we did something just as bizarre and incongruous that was *a matter of habit* before we ate. Dad folded his hands in front of him – his mean, rough, hurting hands with the missing pointer finger and the long, black hairs. And as Dad folded his hands together, this was the cue for all the rest of us to fold our hands together, bow our heads and listen to Dad as he mumbled his mealtime mantra in his southern accent:

*"omosgrashushevnlyfather—thangufothisfood— blesituarnurshmint—fogivarminisins—savusfocrissake— ahmin."*

It took me many years to really be able to decipher exactly *what* Dad was saying. Partly because of how little I was when I first heard this ritual *blessing.* Partly because of Dad's southern accent that slurred the words together – making distinction difficult. But, also, because I didn't hear these words anywhere else. We didn't go to church. We didn't talk about God. Or thank God for anything.

They were just words. Words that were most likely learned by rote and requirement. Words memorized, like the *Pledge of Allegiance,* by Dad as a little boy during the almost two years he spent in the Baptist Orphanage in Jackson, Mississippi. A time when neither of his divorced parents could *or would* take care of him, his three older sisters and his two younger brothers.

Even now, after so many years later, I can still see Dad's hands folded in front of him. I can still hear the words. Only now *I know* the truth of what he was saying, even if there was no real connection of head and heart for him, as he recited his mealtime mantra:

*"O Most Gracious, Heavenly Father, thank you for this food. Bless it to our nourishment. Forgive our many sins. Save us for Christ's sake. Amen."*

Along with Dad's mealtime mantra, there was another *matter of habit* that was maybe even more bizarre and incongruous: We had a ritual bedtime *prayer* – probably learned and memorized by Dad as a little boy, at the same time, in the same place. And familiar to many:

*"Now I lay me down to sleep. I pray the Lord my soul to keep. If I should die before I wake, I pray the Lord my soul to take. God bless Mommy and Daddy and...(here we would insert each of the five names of My Sister, My Three Brothers and me – in descending birth order, of course) ...and God bless everyone. Amen."*

*If I should die before I wake...* That line, said as a *matter of habit*, always stuck in my throat. It always stuck in my mind. There were so many nights that I thought *I would* die. There were so many nights that *I wished* I could die before the morning came.

*If I should die before I wake...* didn't really sound so bad or scary to me. Because dying before I woke up wasn't, *then,* really based on the reality of what it meant for me. It was really just a thought – a magic way – for me to be able to fly away from the *matter of horror* that was lived out in my family.

All pretense of normalcy in my family and all of our daily-day *matter of habit* behaviors could not keep hidden, could not deny and could not stop the ugly-evil-sin of the continuous sexual, emotional and physical abuse – *the matter of horror* – from taking, devouring, poisoning and twisting my mind, my body and my soul.

The ugly-evil-sin wanted all of me...it wanted my all.

# 4

## *...Every inclination of the thoughts of man's heart was only evil all the time*
*Genesis 6:5*

The *whuppin's* and the *beatin's* came. And they came with Dad's ugly anger. His drunkenness. His meanness. His cruelty. His self-centered stupidity. *"I'm gonna be all over you like white on rice!"*

The *whuppin's* and the *beatin's* came with Dad's evil and his hate.

*Why did he hate me? Why did he hurt me? Why did he hurt and hate any of us? Why was he so dangerous? So hateful? So evil? So explosive at any given moment?*

*What did I do to deserve this? Why did he do what he did?*

The *whuppin's* and the *beatin's* came from Dad's hands, just as his ugly, taking touches came.

He would hit with powerful opened-palm slaps – one hand striking right after the other. Smacking my face, my head, my ears, my front, my back, my legs, my bottom. Spinning me, tossing me around. Dad's hands would come at me hard and fast with a cruel anger that was outrageous and inexplicable. And always scary as hell.

*I was helpless. So small. Dad was so much bigger. So dangerous.*

*I want to escape. I want to hide. I want to run. But I can't. It's only done when Dad's done. Like all the hurts he causes.*

The *whuppin's* and the *beatin's* also came from Dad's sudden, back-handed attacks. Striking with such force that his target would often be knocked to the ground.

At the kitchen table, the seat on Dad's right side was called *the hot seat* by us kids. None of us wanted to sit there. Ever. The last kid up to the table would be far worse than just a *rotten egg.*

There was always a lot of scrambling, grabbing for chairs and pushing with elbows to sit anywhere other than in *the hot seat.* The Loser would most likely be the first recipient of Dad's mealtime-madness as his anger exploded from the back of his strong, right, long-black-hair-covered-hand.

One especially destructive night when I was about nine years old, I wasn't fast enough. I had to sit in *the hot seat.* Dad said the mealtime mantra: *omosgrashushevnlyfather* …and the food was passed. Dad's jaw was tightly clenched right from the beginning of the meal. His fingers kept forming, unforming and forming again into a fist. Dad wasn't talking. He was seething just under his silence.

I *tried* to stay quiet. But I wasn't so good at that. Not then. And I could be pretty darn chatty. That particular day I had actually had a really good day in school and thought everybody would just love to hear about it. I was wrong.

No warning came to me. None. Not even a little warning like: *Laney, shut your goddamn mouth.*

I had let my guard down. I was acting as if my family cared about me. About my day. About my life. I was wrong.

Dad's back hand came at me almost fully closed in a fist. But the stump of his trigger finger was still pointed straight out. I caught his eyes just before the blow to the right side of my face twisted me around, throwing me off my chair and into the corner of the trailer.

*He hates me. I see it in his cold, hateful blue eyes. He hates me with a passion that is so overwhelming and frightening. Why do you hate me? Why can't I be happy? Why can't I be a little girl? Why can't I be safe? Why can't I be loved? What did I do? Why do you do this, Dad?*

Dad didn't stop. He leaned over where I landed on the floor and smashed my face hard again. And, then, again.

In one fierce move, Dad picked me up about four feet in the air and threw me with all his force back down against the trailer wall. His right foot and then his left kicked at my sides. I tried to cover my head. The food I had been chewing came spewing out of my mouth. I bit my cheek. I tasted the blood. I tasted the sour chunks coming up from my stomach.

I tried to get away from Dad. Like a frightened little animal, I scurried underneath the table. All the other ten feet belonging to Mom, My Sister and My Three Brothers jumped out of the way as quickly as any feet could move.

I heard Mom call to Dad by his nickname a couple of times, *"Bob! Bob!"* By then all the kids had gotten as far out of the way as possible. But they couldn't go far. We still lived in the trailer. There just wasn't a lot of distance to really get away, even with the addition built on.

And it still wasn't over. Dad's anger had not yet been fully satisfied. He picked up the corner of the yellow formica table, covered with dinner plates, silverware, plastic cups, coffee cups, ashtrays and food. He flipped it on its side throwing it, and everything on it, completely out of his way so he could keep coming at me. And he kept coming. With his fists, his slaps, his long-black-haired-covered-hands, his feet, his hatred, his cruelty.

Dad was crazed. Nothing could stop him. And I had set him off.

*He hates me! How did I make him so angry? What did I do? Hate came from his hands – in every way they could come at me. Hate came from his kicking-stomping feet. Hate welled up from deep within him and flew at me from his eyes. Trying to kill me.*

His eyes were monstrous weapons. Blood veins bursting in the white of his eyes. Unleashed hatred was piercing into me from the cold, evil blue of his eyes.

I begged him, *"Daddy, Stop! Please Stop! I'm sorry, Daddy. I'm sorry! Please Stop! I won't say another word. I promise. Daddy! Please Stop! You're hurting me!"*

His reply spit at me in a voice tightened and possessed with rage, *"I don' give a goddamn! You will learn to shut up if I have to shut you up fo' good! We'll all be a whole hell-uv-a lot better off without your goddamn mouth goin' round here all the goddamn time!"*

Dad didn't stop until I just lay there limp. *It's only done when Dad's done. Like all the hurts he causes. Would I die this time?*

Dad stormed out of the kitchen. But as he went, he opened the high cupboard over the yellow formica counter next to the sink. He grabbed for his bottle of scotch whiskey. But he didn't bother getting one of his usual, short glasses to drink it from. Dad's feet slammed him forward as he pushed through the bedroom-hallway, through the bathroom and, finally, into his bedroom at the end of the trailer. His door was smashed shut. The trailer shook, but just a little. The last I heard from Dad that night was, *"Goddamn stupid, little bitch-uv-a girl! Don' never know when to shut up! Don' never shut her goddamn mouth! Never! She had better goddamn learn to now!"*

I slowly, so slowly, sat up. Rubbing my face, my head, my sides, my back and my legs. Rubbing my left arm. I thought it was broken.

I was so weak. So battered. So dizzy. So sick. So sore. So scared. So tired. So confused. So hated.

And *right then*, it seemed like I was hated by my whole family. I *felt* the hatred and judgment coming at me from Mom, My Sister, My Three Brothers – even though I didn't look up or look around at them. I could imagine each of them thinking – each of them saying in their own minds, *"You should have just kept your big, fat mouth shut! Look what you started tonight!"*

*They were right. Would I ever learn? I had set Dad off. Tonight it was all my fault.*

Keeping silent now, I stood up. But I kept my eyes down. Mom didn't hug me. But she did check my left arm. It was really hanging funny. Mom was a registered nurse, among her other amazing credentials, so she knew what to look for. Mom was able to determine and declare, *"It's not broken."* That's all Mom said.

Nobody else said anything to me.

My Three Brothers were no longer in sight. Mom, My Big Sister and I picked up the disaster zone that was supposed to be our kitchen and our dinner. I tried to be like the *Brownie Elf* and be extra good and extra quick so that I could do the very most for this cleaning-up job. My whole body was hurting so badly. But I knew this was my responsibility.

I also knew that I had better not make any noise. I had better not make *one goddamn peep.* I could stop my words from coming out *now.* Better than I was able to earlier tonight.

But the short, broken-up, rapid-fire sighs came up unbidden from my chest and out my mouth – as I was trying to exhale and catch my breath at the same time. I could not stop my own distorted sighs from coming up. I still can't. Not when I'm upset or tired.

And I could not stop the tears from rolling down my face. Or stop my nose from running. I wiped the tears and snot on my shirt. It didn't matter. It was already such a mess from making Dad so angry.

*I really messed up tonight. Tonight it was all my fault.*

Other times when the *whuppin's* and the *beatin's* came, they just came. Couldn't know whose fault it was. It didn't matter. Knowing wouldn't keep me safe. Knowing wouldn't keep any of us safe from Dad's evil and anger.

It seemed that these *whuppin's* and *beatin's* were given out disproportionately, first, to My Oldest Brother and, then, to me. *We looked more like Dad than the others. Was that why? Did we make Dad see himself too much in our faces? Or maybe in our more fiery personalities? My Oldest Brother and I were also the mouthiest of the five kids. Was that how Dad rationalized his irrational evil, cruelty and hatred of us? Did he lose all sight, all understanding of how very little – how very young – we were when he first started hurting us? Did Dad even really see us at all?*

My Oldest Brother grew more and more solid and strong and angry. As he got a little older, he would fight back with a vengeance – with his words and his fists and his feet. *He was not going to take Dad always treating him like shit. He was not going to be put down and slammed around anymore. Not by Dad! Not by anybody! Goddamn it!*

My Oldest Brother's face would turn a frightening, deep purple-red shade as his anger propelled him towards going completely out of control. Propelled him to physically fight with Dad. To fight for his right not to be *treated like shit.*

But Dad, throughout almost all of our childhood, was still stronger. And he was made even stronger by the constant alcohol and narcotic drugs which flowed evil, twisted power through his blood and his brain. The violent outbursts between the two of them would end when My Oldest Brother's fight was finally beaten out of him by Dad, at least momentarily. And when the blood flowed from his nose or ears, and the welts on his body rose and colored his skin purple and blue, red and black.

The final fight was finally, and for all eternity, out of My Oldest Brother when he died just eleven days after his twenty-fourth birthday. It was a car accident. That was the official report. But, I think he may have been really tired of living with all the evil and hurt he had experienced. And tired of all the evil and hurt he had inflicted on others.

My Oldest Brother had been removed from our home – *as the bad one* – and spent his last two years of high school in a different school district, living between our Grandparents' home and some foster homes. This was so wrong. Mom and Dad were such evil and ugly – and believable – liars. Such masters at covering up the truth. My Oldest Brother was bad and dangerous. That was true. But he never received the love or the help that he needed so desperately here on this earth.

My Oldest Brother had become a drug dealer, then, a drug runner. He had been imprisoned for statutory rape – and couldn't come to my wedding. I really wanted him there, but he had to pay the price of his crime. He also had become involved with a good woman who understood the evil and ugly in this world – and saw it swirling and at times exploding onto her from his out-of-control anger. And through this good woman, My Oldest Brother had become *Daddy* to a beautiful, little girl who was just twenty and one-half months old when he died.

And in between all the ugly and the evil – *because God's grace and truth still speak in the darkest of places* – My Oldest Brother had become a Christian. He always called me his *Jesus Freak Sister*. Even when I called him on his twenty-fourth birthday. Just eleven days before he died. Laughing his very loud laugh, My Big Brother called out to those *hangin'* with him for his birthday, *"Hey, y'all! Give a big shout out to my Jesus Freak Sister!"* And they did!

And I count it a privilege to be a *Jesus Freak* – if that's the name by which I am known for trusting Jesus at His Word. Because it was only by the *freaky* power of God's love and forgiveness that put me, and held me, in a continual and constantly communicating relationship with My Oldest Brother...with *this one* who had wounded and brutalized me so horribly out of his own sick, wounded and brutalized mind, body and spirit.

When it is my turn to die, it will be this same *freaky* power of God's love and forgiveness that will bring My Oldest Brother and me together, once again, to be in an eternal and constantly communing relationship in the presence of our Lord Jesus Christ. *Thank You, my Lord.*

As for me, I first fought back against the insanity happening within our home with my roaring anger. Being *mouthy* like My Oldest Brother, I often had more than just a few *goddamn peeps* finding their way out of my throat. Ever the *Truth-Teller* (This is another BLURSE of my personality. Timing and manner is everything when telling the truth. I didn't know that yet.), I would loudly protest against the things that Dad and Mom did that hurt us and scared us – against the things *that were wrong!*

By age four, not too long after the first time Dad raped me, I made the connection in my little head between Dad's drinking and his hurting us. (I didn't know, yet, about the pills. They didn't stink up his breath.) I wanted Dad's meanness to stop. And I knew I had to do something to stop him from drinking.

So, on a mission – and driven to change things – I climbed onto the yellow, formica kitchen counter, scraping my knees on the ribbed metal trim on my way up. I stood on my tippy toes and reached into the cupboards – between our cereal boxes and our electric blender used for making milkshakes – to pull down two, three or four of Dad's booze bottles. I then sat down on the countertop, just to the left of our sink, and I smashed the first bottle really hard. The glass and booze flew all over. Most of it landed in the sink. There was that smell. That sweet-sick-thick smell that would be on Dad's breath whenever he was too close to me.

Dad and Mom came running in to see what had happened. By then, I had unscrewed the second bottle and was pouring its contents down the kitchen drain. It wasn't going down quickly enough!

Dad madly grabbed the bottle from my two hands and slapped me hard across the face. *"What the hell do you think you are doin'?"*

I was angry and, foolishly, not scared enough just then. I screamed back at him, *"Stop getting drunk! Stop hurting us! Stop touching us! Stop being so mean to us! It's wrong! It's wrong! It's wrong!"*

I scooped up the third bottle determined to dump that one down the sink. Dad ripped *that* bottle out of my grip first, then grabbed me by my shoulders and tossed me to the floor. I jumped right back onto my feet – filled with knowing that I was right and he was wrong! (And filled with way too much adrenaline for my little mind, mouth and body to handle.) Stomping my feet and shaking my fists, I yelled again, *"Dad, you've got to stop hurting us! You've got to stop touching us! You've got to stop getting drunk!"*

*"The only goddamn thing I've gotta do right now is beat the livin' hell outta you!"*

And Dad did.

That was not the only time I would dump Dad's booze bottles. Not surprisingly, however, this behavior didn't exactly win me any *Miss Diplomacy* or *Miss Congeniality* awards. Nor did it stop any of the ugly, sick happenings in my home. But during my earliest years, I was compelled to fight – at least in this small, though totally ineffective (and quite stupid) way. I just had to fight back in some way for myself and for our family. But it didn't stop Dad from hurting us or touching us. It didn't stop Dad from getting drunk. It didn't stop Dad from getting mean. *It's only done when Dad's done. Like all the hurts he causes.*

The *whuppin's* and the *beatin's* came not only from Dad's own hands, fists and feet. Dad also kept an *arsenal* of weapons – belts and branches, knives and razors, rifles and shotguns – that he used against us in his fits of rage as he saw fit.

Dad would unbuckle his belt suddenly and dramatically, and glaring into the eyes of the one to be beaten, pull it quickly, whistling through his belt loops just before the first double-folded crack of *his whip* made contact with our skin. I still hate those sounds. All of them. And I hate the sounds of the screams. From the others. And from me.

Dad's *whuppin's* with his belts left us with welts of puffed flesh, blue and spotted bruising and raised red rips on our bodies. And in our minds.

Dad would have us kids go get branches out of the woods that surrounded our home and bring them back to him to use for our *beatin'*. And *if* those branches did not meet Dad's specification standards for being thick enough, hard enough and hurtful enough, we would have to march ourselves right back into the woods *to fetch a bigger and better branch for our beatin'.*

*Was this all a bizarre and twisted game to Dad? The cruel sickness and controlling evil of Dad permeated everything he seemed to think and do. Did he not have any idea of the damage he was doing to our minds and our bodies? The damage he was doing to our souls? The damage he was doing to his children?*

Dad would pull knives and razors out of his pocket or out of its sheath or out of its case to threaten us, control us and hurt us according to his mood and his judgments.

One early morning when I was seven, I was heading to the backroom of *the addition* to get a dress to wear. We were supposed to have visitors later that day, and I wanted to put on my pretty blue and white checkered dress, with its long ribbons to tie into a bow, its rounded, frilly-collar and its puffy, also frilly, short sleeves.

Mom had made two of these dresses. One for me and another, just a couple of sizes bigger, for My Big Sister. (Which would eventually become my dress too! Hand-me-downs can be so good if the style is cool!) At seven years old, I *really* liked it when My Big Sister and I would wear our look-alike dresses on the same day. She, at eleven, not so much. (*Once I had two daughters of my own, I finally got it.*)

On that early morning, Dad was sitting in his easy chair, handling his hunting knife – almost twirling it, then, using its tip to clean underneath his fingernails. *Gross.* I was in my full slip as I walked past Dad on the only available path to get my dress from the backroom closet – without first going outside through the front door and coming back inside through the backroom door.

Again, without any warning Dad grabbed me. *I thought I was far enough out of Dad's reach. But I never really was. Never. Not ever far enough out of his reach.* Dad grabbed me by my, then, long, beautiful hair. My long, beautiful hair that I loved so much.

He just suddenly yanked my head back by the fistful of my hair he had seized. I tried to pull away, but Dad pulled my hair hard a second time. My head jerked back, I went down to one knee. I tried to stand up again, to get away. I couldn't get free. *It had been such a quiet morning – for those first few moments. I just wanted to get my dress. That's all.*

The first cut from Dad's hunting knife carved off a huge chunk of my hair. Dad pulled my head back again, grabbing at another bunch of my long, beautiful hair and, then, viciously chopping it off with his hunting knife.

I started crying, still trying to get away. *"Daddy, why are you doing this? What did I do? Please, stop, Daddy! Please don't cut my hair!"*

Dad had not said a word until then. He only spoke through his meanness and his weirdly smirking face. Then his voice came declaring his judgment against me: *"You think you're so goddamn high an' mighty. Prancin' 'round here! Thinkin' you're so goddamn much better'n ever'body else. Well, shit! This awtta cut you down to size, Miss Priss!"*

I saw my hair fall. It fell on my shaking chin and on my squished-up, quivering lips. It fell and got stuck to my tear-soaked cheeks. It fell on my slip, on my knees and on my feet. It fell onto the floor. My hair really was long and beautiful. But it wasn't mine anymore.

Another grab. Another hard pull. Another mass of long, beautiful hair was ripped away from my head...away from me. And it continued like this until Dad was done. *It's only done when Dad's done. Like all the hurts he causes.*

And when Dad *was* done, he pushed me hard to the floor to move me out of his way as he got up from his easy chair. I crash landed on a nest of hair that wasn't mine anymore.

Dad walked into the kitchen, calling out to Mom as he went, *"Vivian, you better git out the hair-cuttin' scissors. Goddamn it if Laney don't needs a bit of fixin' up b'fo' our company gits here!"*

*Where was Mom before? Why didn't she stop it? Why can nothing be beautiful here? Why can nothing be mine? Not even my hair? Why is everything ruined? And taken and destroyed? I hate my family! I hate it here! I hate my hair! I hate myself!*

I didn't wait for Mom to *git out the hair-cuttin' scissors.* I ran outside – but just before I did, I reached out and placed my hand on the gigantic, red, *family* Bible (that had belonged to Mom's grandparents) that no one in my family ever read. It sat centered on the second level of the bookshelf close to where Dad had been sitting in his easy chair. It was at least four inches thick. And resting on its back, I could easily read its fancy, gold, scripted letters: *Holy Bible.* It was big and heavy and strong. I just wanted to touch it and feel its velvety, red surface and the indent of its title – and say a quick prayer to God to help me. Time stood still for those few seconds.

Just a few weeks before my long, beautiful hair had all been chopped off, I had been given my own Bible and taught a little bit about prayer from some nice people at a one week camp. So, before I ran from this place – where Dad had, once again, ripped part of me away – I just wanted to touch this big, heavy, strong Bible.

Then, I ran. I headed straight into the woods. To disappear. In my slip. With no shoes and very little hair left. I leaned into one of our beautiful, white birch trees that grew alongside so many other stronger, sturdier trees throughout our woods. I rubbed my right hand over one of the oval, dark and exposed areas that spotted its trunk. I rubbed my left hand over my head, a few more loose strands of hair floated to the ground. I felt so dark and exposed. And I cried. I slid down to the base of the trunk. And I cried some more. And I whispered some more prayers.

I didn't stay there too long. I knew I'd be in even bigger trouble if I didn't let Mom do *a bit of fixin' up* on my hair *b'fo' our company gits here!*

When I went back inside the house, Mom had the scissors out and ready. She had me stand on the little stool in front of the bathroom mirror. Mom gave me my first *Pixie* haircut.

That's what she called it. She told me I would look fine. I just stood there numb. And silent. *I wasn't me anymore.*

Dad did not lash out only at me when it came to *cuttin' hair*. He was absolutely brutal, shaming and violently controlling as he *cut* My Oldest Brother and My Big Brother's hair. Cutting deeply into their minds and souls by his hateful cruelty at the same time.

Dad would *punish* the two of them for their disrespectful behavior – according to his own determination of what was respectful or disrespectful behavior towards him. (Dad demanded absolute and immediate obedience from all of us. And our responses to him had better be spoken with a clear *"Yessir"* or *"No-sir"* whenever addressing him.)

Dad's punishment-torture-*haircuts* began by dragging My Brothers, one at a time, into the bathroom by the fistful of hair Dad had grabbed onto from the tops of their heads. Dad would hold them in a vise-like grip with his left arm around their neck or head and with his right hand he would quickly and viciously dig his razor deep into their heads.

Shaving off their hair, cutting it completely off. Cutting down into their scalps. My Two Older Brothers were both big, burly, muscular boys, even from an early age. But nothing could stop Dad. Nothing could stop his violent rages. Not then. *It's only done when Dad's done. Like all the hurts he causes.*

*And then there were the guns.* Shotguns and rifles meant for hunting – that Dad would tear down off the racks, fully loaded, cock the trigger and shoot. The bullets flew whizzing just past our ears, flying just over our heads or exploding into the ground right at our feet as we ran. Dad would hold the barrel to one of our *goddamn heads*, screaming out his hate, screaming out his threats to us, *"I'm gonna git rid of you fo' good. An' good goddamn riddance!"*

Dad did *"git rid of fo' good"* our dog, Tanya Two. *This* Tanya was almost identical in looks and sweet nature to our first Tanya who had died when hit by a car just before we moved to Connecticut for those two years. *This* Tanya took to sleeping underneath the bottom bunk too. Sometimes with me joining her when I was scared or sad or numb. I joined her a lot.

I don't know what Tanya did. But Dad was angry. Screaming at her for being a *"stupid, goddamn bitch-uv-a dog! Doesn't listen to a goddamn thing she's told!"* Dad kicked her hard in her rear-quarters. Tanya crouched as low as she could possibly go and still be able to move. With her tail pushed far down under her bottom she crawled underneath the bottom bunk to get away from Dad. But Dad wasn't done with her.

He got down on all fours himself. Like an animal. Dad grabbed Tanya by her collar and dragged her whimpering –

but not too loudly, she knew better – down the hall. Tanya's pleading brown, wet eyes met mine. I think she was crying. I know she was scared. Me too.

Just before forcing Tanya outside, Dad reached for his rifle. *"You kids, git your faces up thar to that kitchen window! Right now, goddamn it! An' jus' watch what happens when I'm not listened to!"*

Fear of Dad – fear for Tanya – moved us up to the kitchen window that ran almost the entire width of the trailer's front end.

Dad's tight hold on Tanya's collar was only released when he slammed her side one more time with a powerful kick from his right foot clad in his brown, hard-rubber-trimmed work boot. Tanya went flying. And even before she landed on the ground, Dad had his rifle cocked and aimed. She landed hard. A yelp flew out from her lungs just as she hit the ground. Just as the first bullet pierced into them.

One, Two. Three. Four more shots were pummeled into Tanya's already badly beaten body. I can still hear the bullets' exploding noise. I can still hear Tanya's howling cries after each of the first three shots entered her body. She didn't make a sound for the last two.

*(I've only had one full-blown, totally irrational panic attack in my life. I'm thinking that's pretty darn good, considering some of my circumstances. We were living in France at the time. On Bastille Day, we decided to take our two small daughters, some family guests and their two young children to Paris. We didn't realize what a stupid thing that was to do. As we came up onto the street level of the Champs Élysées from the underground subway, we were surrounded by absolute insanity. A mass of people*

gone wild immediately swallowed us up. The noise was unbelievable. Loud, raucous shouting. Rapid bursts of firecrackers exploding all around us. One landed right underneath my baby's stroller. I moved her out of the way as quickly as I could. The sound was too much like gunfire. The people were too out of control. I lost it. I just totally lost it. I burst into tears. And into hysteria. I could barely breathe. I shouted to Tim, "We've got to get out of here now!" I grabbed our three year old daughter by the hand and ferociously pushed the stroller holding our one year old daughter through the crowd – sobbing, shaking, shouting at the terrible, stupid people for endangering my babies, my family and me. A flood of adrenaline shoved me back down underground. Back to safety. Back to where the people were not crazy. Back to where the explosions were not attacking.)

Boom. Boom. Boom. Boom. Boom. I hated those noises from Dad's gun – from Dad's evil. I had been standing on my tip toes on one of the kitchen chairs pressed up against the window to watch – to obey Dad – as he murdered Tanya. Not one of us kids said anything. We were crying. My Big Brother probably loudest of all. My Oldest Brother's face was tighter than ever, with jaws clenched and his eyes fiery with rage and rimmed with tears ready to pour out. My Big Sister held onto My Little Brother. They were both shaking, lips quivering, tears flowing.

I was crying hard – but not too loudly, I knew better. I was so sick. I knew I'd be throwing up again soon. I always threw up. And I just kept thinking: *I hate him. I hate him. I hate him. I hate him. I hate him. I hate him.*

Dad's face turned to stare in at us kids through the kitchen window as if to say, *"That should teach y'all a lessin. You listen to me when I say sumthin'! An' y'all better do what I say when I say it the first goddamn time!"* He took Tanya's dead body by the collar, dragging her off somewhere. To bury her? To throw her into the woods?

And I just kept thinking: *I hate him. I hate him. I hate him. I hate him. I hate him. I hate him.*

One gun-night of terror (among so many) is so deeply ingrained in my brain that it's as if each scene had been preserved in the full magic of Technicolor made known to the world and to me during the Sunday night TV show, *Walt Disney's Wonderful World of Color.*

We're all outside. Behind the trailer. All in our jammies ...or at least parts of them. The air is fresh and cool. Flowers, trees and earth smells surround me and fill my nose. The night sky is so beautiful, big and black, and laden and lit by the huge, round, almost touchable moon and by the brightly shining, countless stars – either standing alone or joining others in their magnificent constellations.

But we aren't out here to take in this awesome beauty. We're out here because of the awful ugly that has taken over us.

Dad is so drunk. So crazed. It's Mom's turn to be the hunted. He had chased her out of the trailer with his gun. Fear from the screaming and hitting sounds of Dad's violence had gripped all of us kids and tore us all out of our beds and out to behind the trailer in the middle of the night.

Mom is wearing her just-below-the-knees, soft, pink nightgown. It has a V-neck with ties at the top of the collar so that it makes almost a diamond shape when she ties it. But it's not tied tonight. It's undone. Mom's hair is all messy. She's more frightened than I've ever seen her. She doesn't even have her glasses on. She must have had to run away from Dad hitting and hurting her without any time to put them on. Or maybe Dad had knocked them off her face.

*Oh, Mom. Not being able to see clearly must make all of this night that much more ugly, distorted, evil and confusing to you. I wish I could go get your glasses for you. I would, Mom. But Dad's so dangerous right now. The gun is so scary. I can't go in and get them for you. I'm so sorry.*

Dad is holding the barrel of his rifle right at Mom's head. He is bigger and meaner than ever. The evil blue of his eyes can be seen, even now, on this well-lit night of darkness. Dad is completely out of his mind. Threatening and yelling, *"Goddamn you, Vivian! I am sick an' tar'd of puttin' up with all this shit from you an' from all of those goddamn kids! I'd be better off if y'all wuz dead! Every goddamn last one of you!"*

Mom is cowering up against the back end of the trailer. She is so scared. She's trying to see. But I know she can't. Not well. Almost not at all. Not with her tears streaking down her face and the terror shaking her entire body. No. She can't *see* well. But Mom can *feel* the barrel of the gun pressing into her temple as she tries to press herself into the back end of the trailer and away from Dad.

Mom's calling out, *"Bob! Bob, for God's sake! Stop this! Please! Stop this! Bob, you're scaring me! You're scaring the kids! Bob, let me help you. Put the gun down, Bob! Please!"*

I call out. The other kids call out. Some of us are pleading. Some of us are crying. Some of us are filled with hate. Some of us are filled with terror. Maybe all of us. In all of those ways. We all call out.

"Daddy, please don't hurt Mommy! Please don't hurt her! Put the gun down, Daddy! Please stop! Please stop, Daddy!"

And the gun is turned on us. Dad opens then slams shut the cock, ready to shoot. And we run. Fast. Down through the back field. Past the enormous vegetable garden we planted. Running on the path cut through the woods. Down to the river. The moon and the stars help us see. Our fear, our anger, our tears do not.

The gun fires. Mom screams.

*Do I keep running? What happened? What is happening? This is so crazy! This is so awful! Why are we like this? Why am I always afraid? Why is there so much evil? Why is there so much hate? Do I turn around? Do I go check on Mom? I can't stop running. I feel like I'm flying, but I know I'm touching the ground. My feet are getting slippery from the night's wet grass. Little clumps of dirt are splattered all over my legs, way up to above my knees. I'm so scared. Is Mom okay? I hate this! I'm so alone. How can that be? There are five of us kids. But we all seemed to scatter and hide, move forward, clear obstacles, stop or turn back – all of us on our own private trajectories.*

*(This was true of each of us on our separate paths for healing too.)*

And then, an even louder scream. This time it's Dad. The scream comes almost as a roar of unbearable pain. Of fear. Of evil. Of shock. All rolling and twisting together as Dad's scream bursts out from the depths of his body, mind and soul. His cry pierces this once beautiful, now horribly evil and ugly, night. And it pierces and sears every fiber of my being.

I run back. Fast. I'm not brave. I'm worried. All of us run back. But we don't huddle together. We just look on from our separate watching posts. The gun is on the ground where Dad had been standing. Mom, who was shaking with terror before, is now on her knees holding Dad. He's on his knees too, crumpled up against her, pressed into her chest and sobbing. Mom is rocking Dad. He is now the one shaking uncontrollably.

We all stayed in our places. So did the stars and the moon. They were still beautiful. We weren't.

Mom uses the back end of the trailer to help balance and steady her as she helps Dad to his feet. Dad is bent and leaning into Mom for support – their arms around each other's waists. Dad is making sobbing, sniffling sounds and saying, *"I'm sorry, Viv. I'm sorry. I'm sorry…"*

They slowly walk forward towards the back door of the addition. Mom turns halfway around, *"You kids go on to your beds. Get to sleep. Daddy will be okay now. It's all done now."*

I was filled with so many thoughts. I *do* want Dad to be okay. I *do* want it to be all done. But I didn't really believe it. So much anger and fear and evil and hate and collapse had all just taken place. And *now* it was done? I felt like I was spinning. I just sat down on the wet grass behind the trailer. I still couldn't move. Too much numbness. Too many thoughts. I didn't trust that it was done.

And it wasn't. Not yet. Not for many, many years. *It's only done when Dad's done. Like all the hurts he causes.*

And Dad was only done for that one night.

# 5

## *As long as the earth endures, seedtime and harvest, cold and heat, summer and winter, day and night will never cease*

*Genesis 8:22*

There were some nights that were more peaceful than others. When the screams were stilled. The fear was never far away, but some nights I could just sleep. I liked that. Nobody woke me up for anything. No touching me. No scaring me. No running. Just sleep. Those nights were good.

I love the sound of crickets and other night bugs making their clicking-clacking and humming sounds. I love the sound of rain coming down hard against windows, roofs and walls. And I especially love the sound of rain drumming and splashing against tin metal, as it did against our trailer.

Those were the night sounds I was able to hear whenever the fear and anger, hurt and hate were silenced for a time. Those are still the sweet, safe, take-a-deep-breath, sleep-in-peace sounds to my ears…to my heart, to my mind and to my soul.

As parents, Tim and I always had our own nightly ritual with our precious little girls, Erin and Julia. Of course, part of that nightly ritual was made up by the requisite bath time and book time and another-glass-of-water-time and just-one-more-hug-time. The other part of our nightly ritual, for all their growing up years, was what we called our *Prayers and Thankfuls.*

We would gather in our daughters' room and together share at least one *Thankful* we wanted to thank God for about that day. Some days our *Thankfuls* flowed – as we enjoyed the good stuff that was going on at home, at school, at work, at church, with friends, with all their music activities...maybe there was some kind of celebration – a birthday party, an anniversary, a prom, a graduation, a wedding, a vacation, a holiday, a big, beautiful snowfall (especially fabulous if it caused a school closing), a perfect summer day at the beach, a day at *Disney's Magic Kingdom.* Some days our *Thankfuls* trickled – as we dealt with an illness, a hole in Julia's heart, bone tumors in Erin's jaw, a surgery, waiting for a biopsy, the hurt of rejection by a friend, by a boss, by a boy, by a college...maybe we just had a really cruddy day...and an even cruddier attitude to go along with it. But no matter how tough that day might have been, we still came together to share our *Thankfuls* with each other and with God.

And then, we said our *Prayers* together, first taking turns talking out loud to God, mentioning specific people and their circumstances that we felt needed an extra measure of God's love and help in their lives right then. Julia, as a very little girl, would always close her personal prayers with, *"Amen for me."* Then as a foursome, we would close with our own – more *life*-focused – unison prayer than what I had learned as a child: *"Now I lay me down to sleep. I pray the Lord my soul to keep. Guide me safely through the night, and wake me with the morning light. God bless Mommy and Daddy and Erin and Julia (...then each and every family member – from both sides of our family were prayed for by their names)...and God bless EV-ER-Y-ONE! In Jesus' name, Amen!"*

So many nights after tucking our Erin and Julia into their beds and after sharing our *Prayers and Thankfuls,* Tim and I would walk down the hall, arms around each other's waists and I would, more often than not, fill up with tears. And those tears would run down my cheeks as my heart and my head were filled and flowing with so many more *Thankfuls* to our God.

Two specific times that those *Thankful* tears *danced* down my cheeks were, first, when the cardiologist announced that *the hole in our, then, four year old Julia's heart had completely and spontaneously (by God's power) closed up on its own – leaving no evidence that her heart ever had a hole in it!* (This is such tangible evidence of what the mighty power of God's love can do to heal each of our own hearts completely – emotionally and spiritually!) And a second, specific time (among numerous times) when *Thankful* tears *danced* down my cheeks, was just four months before our Erin graduated from college. The bone tumors in Erin's jaw – for which she had needed several surgeries since she was in third grade and which had destroyed her permanent teeth on her left jaw – were finally determined to be permanently dormant! No more destruction! Now the restoration could be done! (Again! This is such tangible evidence of what the mighty power of God's love can do to stop everything that would destroy us and, then, bring to us His full, loving restoration and renewal for our lives!)

Our little girls knew peace. They did not know abuse. They did not know terror. They slept in peace. No evil, no fear, no screams disturbed their sleep. God had given me a new life. And God had given me – given to us – a family that knew His love. And the three of us – God, Tim and I – were going to do everything we possibly could to keep it that way for those two beautiful, little girls…and for us. And I thanked our God. And I thanked and hugged my Tim.

And just as there were some nights during my childhood that were more peaceful than others, there were also some days when the fear and ugly, the anger and hurt were a bit quieter. There were some days that were even sweet and fun and good.

That's because *antinomy* has always existed. *Antinomy* is a great word, and a word that God has used to help me understand the seemingly bizarre and oppositional truths that can exist at the same time, in the same life, and within the same person.

In the *Webster's Encyclopedic Unabridged Dictionary of the English Language* (Yes, I'm a nerd. I have my own personal copy of this fabulously gigantic, word-explaining book. It's one of the most dog-eared books in my possession after my Bible(s) and two of my other, equally gigantic and information-filled books: *Strong's Exhaustive Concordance of the Bible* and *Matthew Henry's Commentary on the Whole Bible*. Yes, I really am a nerd.), the meaning of *antinomy* is: "1) opposition between one law, principle, rule, etc., and another. 2) a contradiction between two statements, both apparently obtained by correct reasoning."

Or more easily stated: *Antinomy* is when two very different truths are true at the same time.

And there were always two very different truths existing within my childhood. It's just that for a very long time, it was the poison of the ugly and hurtful, evil and hateful that won out most of the time over those fewer, and far less dramatic, peaceful, sweet, fun and good times. But they did both exist. The antinomy within my family – the poison and the peace – always coexisted...twistedly coexisted together.

Those days that were good, where the memories still bring me a smile and even a laugh, almost always took place outside...or, at least, started there.

Mom and Dad were both hard workers, and we kids similarly, and necessarily, learned to work hard. And outside, our huge vegetable garden required a lot of hard work and a lot of our time. I didn't mind the work or the time because being busy and purposeful can be *a-whole-heck-of-a-lot-better* than a lot of other things that went on in my family. So, outside-garden-work-days were mostly good days.

The spring garden work began with Dad driving his big yellow, rusty tractor to plow up the ground – turning the hard earth that had been stomped down and compressed by Lake Ontario's heavy winter snows – to make it open itself up to the seeds we would plant. And taking turns up beside Dad on the tractor's wide and bumpity seat, each of us five kids got a chance *to drive.* Then would come the planting of the, *oh-my-goodness*, such long garden rows. We would all be out there, all seven of us – at varying times – to first make little holes in the ground, then to plop the seeds down into those holes, and finally to bury the seeds under little mounds of rich, brown earth. We'd also collect any wiggly worms we could find, putting them in our worm-and-night-crawler-buckets, for some *fishin'* at the river later.

In the late summer and early fall would come the *pickin'* of all that burst out of our garden. One unusually, almost magical, sun-shiny, blue-sky day (a rare occurrence along Lake Ontario's cloudy, southeastern shore), I was out *pickin'* peas – all plump and green – in the same row as Dad, right across from him. As we picked and plucked, I told Dad all about *Peter Pan.* Not too long before this magical day, we had (as a family) watched this imagination-capturing, taped-for-television, Broadway Musical version of *Peter Pan* starring Mary Martin.

I had found my soul mate in *Peter Pan*! Flying, singing …escaping from the world of grown-ups! Oh! What could be better?! After watching that show, I knew everything about *Peter Pan.* So, I proceeded to tell Dad, while *pickin'* peas, everything I knew about Peter and Wendy and John and Michael and Mr. and Mrs. Darling and Nana – the Nursemaid-Dog and Tinker Bell and Fairy Dust and Captain Hook and Smee and all of the other Pirates and Princess Tiger Lily and the Indians and the Lost Boys and…

And the sweet and good thing is that on *that* day – on *that* magical, sun-shiny, blue-sky day – my Dad listened to me. He looked at me. Dad looked into my blue eyes that matched the color of his blue eyes that matched the color of the sky *that* day. Dad listened to me and Dad looked at me and Dad smiled at me and Dad laughed with me. I must have been so ridiculously silly, and probably more than a little bit crazy-making, as I told Dad – with great dramatic flair and enthusiastically *singin'* every single song – absolutely everything I knew and loved about *Peter Pan*.

And on *that* day, I had a very good, pea-pickin', *Peter Pan* day with my Dad.

I know Dad remembered it too, because when he was telling his *good* stories to company – not his *bitchin' an' moanin'* stories or his hate-filled stories – Dad would tell about that pea-pickin', *Peter Pan* day when I just couldn't tell him enough about *Peter Pan*…and what a *Chatty Cathy* I was! Dad even told Tim this story when we were dating (and quite a few more times after we were married). Whenever Dad told it, Dad would smile. And Dad would laugh. I think we were both pretty happy that we, at least, had *that* day…that *pea-pickin'* good day. And I thank God for it often.

Most of the other days that I considered good with Dad, were actually days without Dad.

Dad was in and out…and in and out…of hospitals for all kinds of surgeries and rehabilitation programs – usually stemming from the mid-1960's accident that disabled him when a tree fell across his back while he was down in a ditch welding a pipeline together. Other times Dad went into the hospital because he had taken a fall off the roof while *shinglin'* it or fallen into the river while *fishin'* or he had over-dosed on a combination of his prescription narcotics and booze – both to which he was horribly addicted. The busyness of the surgical wards, the boredom of the waiting rooms, the narrow hallways with black and white patterned linoleum floors, the cover-up disinfectant smells, the not-very-soft-white hospital sheets and the warn-thin blue hospital gowns are well ingrained in my memory banks from visiting Dad so many times in the Syracuse, New York hospitals.

Some of Dad's days away from home were also spent in and out...and in and out...of another kind of hospital: the psychiatric hospital at Marcy. I only visited Dad there a couple of times as a child. We always visited him there while sitting outside on a bench or at a little table. But only when the weather was warm.

Other days, Dad would *just up and leave* home for extended periods of time, especially after he could no longer work even part-time due to his physical and mental health. One of those times Dad left was when I was very ill and had to have emergency surgery myself. It seemed especially bizarre to me that Dad would have left *this* time because, just the day before my surgery, it had been Dad who had come to pick me up from school. He even took me for a quick (although diagnostically useless) trip to a local doctor on *that* day when I could no longer hide how very sick I was. (*Tim, my best friend at the time but not yet my boyfriend, had actually been the one who helped me to get from study hall up to the nurse's office. I thanked him by throwing up all over him in a very tightly enclosed stairwell. He married me five years later, anyway. Now, if that's not love, I just don't know what is!*) Up to that point, I hadn't told anyone how sick I was or how much pain I'd been feeling. I just didn't want to deal with either being ignored or being the one to increase the drama level at my home. So, I just stayed quiet about feeling so sick.

The morning after Dad picked me up from school, I woke up to a blinding fever and such crippling abdominal pain that I could not walk. Dad was not home. Mom was at work. My Brothers were at school. But! My Big Sister was there! She hadn't left yet for her classes – she was studying to become a licensed practical nurse. And she was the *right* one to be with me right then. My Big Sister drove me to the emergency room of the nearest hospital. She called Mom who arrived just moments after we did. Within an unbelievably short and exceedingly blurry time, I was prepped for surgery. Only it wasn't my appendix, as we all had expected – it was my ovaries.

When I woke in the recovery room, Mom and My Big Sister were looking very serious and speaking very gently and quietly. The surgeon had removed my entire right ovary – describing it as th*e size of a basketball,* and along with it, he had removed my right fallopian tube and three-quarters of my left ovary – describing that one as being *the size of a grapefruit.* (How did all that fit inside of me?)

When the doctor came to check in on me, he also was serious and gentle, but not too quiet, as he explained that my "*ovaries and fallopian tube were in a stage of pre-cancerous growth and completely covered and enveloped in cysts.*" Yuck. He went on, Mom and My Big Sister were listening to the doctor intently and looking at me sadly, "*We will need to start you on a regimen of hormones,*" (I thought, *okay.* That's not too bad.) "*and this will most likely mean that you will not be able to have children of your own.*" At that moment in time that didn't bother me. I was only fifteen.

*(And since years later, even with only one-quarter of one of my ovaries remaining, Tim and I did have children of our own, our beautiful Erin and Julia, God obviously had a very different prognosis in mind than did my doctor! And I'm so glad God did!)*

Dad never came to the hospital. I was so drugged up most of the time I was only barely aware of who came and went. But Dad didn't come.

When I got home from the hospital, Dad had already *up and left*. His usual place to go during his extended *missing in action* times was to Mississippi. He went down there to visit his family...to go *back down home*. Very few of Dad's numerous southern kinfolk ever made the trip up north to visit us at our home.

Mom's parents, my Grandma and Grandpa, were the only grandparents I ever really knew and spent time with while growing up. They lived just a few towns over from us. Grandma and Grandpa are a big part of my good day memories – and part of the antinomy of my family. Again, most of these good day memories took place outside or, at least, outside our home. As kids, all five of us would go *at the same time* to spend a couple of nights at their trailer home in Volney, NY – and almost always during the Volney Firemen Field Days. Both Grandpa and Grandma were very involved in the fire department as a fireman and ladies' auxiliary member – just as they had been in the town where I grew up. *(Before they moved to Volney, My Grandparents actually sold their home to Tim's parents when Tim was only two years old. This was the same house that Mom had moved into when she was eleven years old...and the same house where, at twenty-one, she met Dad. He was renting a room from My Grandparents while he worked on the local area pipelines. This was the same house where Tim grew up...and the house that holds many special memories from our dating years...this was the house where Tim's Mom and Dad hosted holidays, our wedding rehearsal dinner and welcomed their first grandchildren. These kinds of connections can, and quite often do, happen in a small town.)*

With Grandma and Grandpa, our whole family would spend one summer week up at Racquette Lake in the Adirondack Mountains at the *camp* owned by my Grandpa's cousin. This Racquette Lake *camp* had once been the *Racquette Lake Hotel*, reminding me a bit of the *Shady Rest Hotel* from the 1960's sitcom, *Petticoat Junction*. It was big and quirky with a number of areas where I could have a little bit of space...have a little bit of quiet all to myself. Up there, all the mountain and lake activities – hiking, swimming, canoeing, water-skiing – sang out to my inner tomboy, my inner *Peter Pan*...while the natural beauty of this place sang out to my inner Princess. Going to Racquette Lake with My Grandparents as witnesses also helped to keep *most* – but not all and not all of the time – of the ugly and evil away from us whenever we stayed there. Oh, it really was good to be in that place.

And the good days with Mom were often started outside, but usually finished in the kitchen. We kids would take big buckets out into the patches of wild growing berries – strawberries, raspberries and blackberries – that sprang up around our home and just across and down the road a bit. And we would pick and eat these free, sweet treats until both our buckets and bellies were full.

Then, we would do with these berries just as we did with the vegetables grown in our garden and the apples and pears that grew in our own little orchard. We would bring the abundance of garden and bush, tree and vine into the kitchen to Mom.

And Mom, as Master of the Kitchen tirelessly doing most of the work herself, would expertly orchestrate the work we five kids would do in order to help clean, cut, can and freeze just about everything that the seven of us would be eating as our fruits and vegetables over the next several months. Anything that we didn't eat up immediately found its way into the tightly packed deep-freeze or into a canning jar before it could spoil. Nothing was wasted.

I especially liked making jellies with Mom. Mostly because I really liked to eat them! Mom taught me about the paraffin she covered all of her jellies with – just after she filled up the pretty, diamond-shaped-decorated, little glass jelly jars and before sealing them shut with the brassy-gold colored, little-lipped-lids. (Mom didn't use the mason jars with their special screw-on-tops and funny looking, hinged sealing mechanism for her jellies. Those were for her tomatoes, tomato sauce, chili-pepper sauce, pickles and such.)

Mom would let me play and make funny shapes with the extra little bits of the warm paraffin wax while we worked. I got to help with washing the berries, cooking them down, adding the sugar, stirring and tasting. Mom was usually happy when she canned and cooked. I liked it when Mom was happy. She seemed less distant then. We could talk about what we were cooking, how it was coming along and what still needed to be done. Those were our most intimate talking times when I was little – just talking about what we were cooking. We both liked to cook and we both liked to eat pretty much everything we cooked. I still do.

Mom's blackberry jelly was my absolute favorite of all the jellies she canned. After Mom died, I asked Dad if I could check the cellar to see if there were any left. Just a few jars remained on the shelves that had once been stocked to feed a family of seven. I took one precious jar of Mom's blackberry jelly home. Back to my own family – to share it and savor it.

Erin and Julia were just eight and six years old when Mom died at fifty-nine. They weren't ready to hear *all* the truths of my life. They weren't ready to hear, or even begin to understand, the *antinomy* of my Mom's – their Grandma's – life. But they could taste and experience the sweet, dark, chunky-but-seedless blackberry jelly that their Grandma was an expert at making. And with Tim, the four of us slathered that blackberry jelly onto our warm, buttered toast, enjoying every bite, licking our fingers and making all sorts of *yummy* sounds. (Well, I was making *yummy* sounds, anyway.) And while we ate our blackberry jellied toast and drank our glasses of extra cold milk, I told my precious ones stories of buckets and bellies filled with blackberries and all the steps it takes to make the best jelly in the world. That only my Mom could make.

And I cried when there was no more left. Mom was done making blackberry jam. I was done tasting that sweet part of the *antinomy* of her life.

Mom was not only present and busy and very good at what she did in the kitchen; she was also very good at the work she did outside the home. And her work, although very demanding, always seemed to make her happy. Happier than being at home.

Mom was one of the most intelligent people I have ever known in my entire life. (*Antinomy*, remember.) She had been a top scholar in high school and at the University of Rochester where she earned her B.S. Degree as a registered nurse. After our two year interlude of inner city living in

East Hartford, CT, Mom began working as a case worker for the Department of Social Services in our County – where she earned great respect and well deserved promotions. Over the years, Mom also worked as Director of Nursing for a well regarded nursing home. (My high school psychology class actually took a field trip there – with the educational tour led by Mom. I know! *Antinomy*.)

On a few winter days, when the schools were closed because of blowing, drifting and mounting snow and many of her staff could not make it in due to the weather, Mom would ask me if I would go with her to help out with her elderly patients at the nursing home. I always said, *"Yes ma'am."* Work, we could do together. This was our way of communicating – our way of connecting. We were both hard workers. And we were similar in heart when it came to caring for people. I saw that especially in the way Mom helped people outside our home. Or in the way Mom attended to us when we were really sick or physically hurt by something or someone...*other than Dad.*

Mom's gentleness, caring and sense of humor really came through during my ovarian surgery ordeal. Just before I went into surgery, Mom asked if I wanted anything. I said, *"Yes, please. A lemon lollipop and a Big Mac."* For me, it was actually spelled as *Big Mack*. I already liked Tim Mack *a lot*, and Mom knew that we were good friends. I think she got it. She gave me a big, twinkly-eyed smile. The next day Mom came in with my lemon lollipop. Then giggling, she pulled out a stuffed toy in the shape of a giant hamburger with a full face, legs and feet, arms and hands to go along with its *two all beef patties, special sauce, lettuce, cheese, pickles, onions, on a sesame seed bun.* Its tag introduced my stuffed hamburger to me as *Big Mack*. Mom gave me another big, twinkly-eyed smile. And as I hugged my *Big Mack* to my heart, I gave a big, twinkly-eyed (and a little drugged-up) smile right back to Mom. And we laughed. I let Mom know that I really did like Tim Mack. She already knew. If for no other reason, I am so thankful to have gone through this awful illness and surgery because it gave Mom and me some sweet, silly and intimate moments that I hold so very special and close to my heart...to this day. And I thank God for those moments.

Mom and I were also quite similar in our attitude and approach toward driving. We both liked to drive. We're not easily intimidated by bad weather – which can really translate out to mean a lack of wisdom-infused caution or having way too much confidence in our driving abilities ...or being just a little bit *nuts*. And we both liked to drive *fast*. I believe I inherited Mom's heavy, *lead foot* on the gas pedal. A friend once warned me, "*Do NOT drive any faster than your guardian angels can fly!*" Point taken. I'm a law-abiding citizen *now* and, dutifully and necessarily, turn on my cruise control to help me where I lack self-control. At least, most of the time.

Mom's last two jobs clearly showed the *antinomy* of her life. She worked as (holding both positions simultaneously) the Director of Nursing at the Mental Health Center for our County and as the Town Court Justice (an elected position) where she and Dad lived – where I had grown up. Mom was truly the brilliant, hardworking, caring, authoritative, well respected, leader woman that almost all people outside our home knew her to be. *And* Mom was just as truly the victim and the perpetrator, the captive and the accomplice of the horrendous and hidden emotional, physical and sexual abuse that went on inside our home.

On one of my brief summer visits home while I was in college, I was in the car with Mom heading, first, into our town and, then, out of town on our way to the nursing home where she worked. Mom was short-staffed that summer day due to employee vacation time rather than the usual culprit that came in the form of a winter blizzard. As we drove away from home, the same river that ran behind our house also wound its way to the edge of the village making it necessary to cross *The Little Bridge* (*The Big Bridge* was in the opposite direction). In order to go almost anywhere for anything we had to cross *The Little Bridge*.

That day as we crossed over *The Little Bridge* – the bridge Mom crossed to go to work and the bridge Mom crossed to go back home – Mom spoke these words, not with a lot of emotion, but with a deep tiredness of voice and soul...not looking at me, but looking at *The Little Bridge*: *"When I cross this bridge to go to work, my life begins. And when I cross this bridge to go back home, my life ends."*

My heart broke for Mom and all that meant on so many levels. I reached out to touch Mom's hand gently... carefully...thoughtfully. We did touch for a few seconds. Mom, then, reached her same hand over to pick up her cigarette, rimmed with the deep red color of her lipstick. She took a long drag on it. No more words. Mom had let me in just a little bit, and then retreated. She turned on the radio. I turned my head to look out the window as I turned to God in prayer, asking God, once again, to *please heal my family.*

The natural changing of times and seasons...*of seedtime and harvest...of day and night*...came and went over the years. And I knew what to expect from them and, usually, knew how to prepare for them. But for the changing moods and changing danger levels in my home, although I had come to expect their sudden shifts, I was never really quite prepared for them when they hit. Not fully. I kept myself on guard, but never enough. I was a kid. And so, the *antinomy* – the twisted mix of the poison and the peace – in my home and within my family confused me and created a constant fault line in my head...with the pressure building as I tried to prepare myself for the next earthquake of the ugly and the evil to erupt.

# 6

## *In my anguish I cried to the LORD...*
### *Psalm 118:5*

On my *own* good days as a little girl, I would most often be *alone*. I would go off riding my bike – even as far as to the bluffs that looked out on Lake Ontario or as far as Selkirk Shores State Park, about seven miles away. And once I arrived there, I would still walk all the way to the very end of the pier to feel the wind and the water splash... to hear the gulls calling and the waves crashing...to smell the fish and the long, green, heavy strands of seaweed that clung to the sides of the pier.

Alone, I would go hiking in our woods, climbing in our trees, walking down to the river and sitting there on my favorite Big Rock...talking to Jesus. Just like He was right there with me. And if I wasn't riding or running in some way, I would be reading – sitting crossed-legged on the corner of my bed or up against a tree or on the porch at the Racquette Lake camp – reading books like the Greek classics and myths given to me by my Grandpa or reading one of the seventy-two *Bobbsey Twins* books. Or, even more often, I would be alone reading my Bible that was given to me from that one week summer camp I had gone to. Even at age seven when I got it, that Bible was talking to me. Early on I realized that God, at least according to the

Bible, also wanted me to talk with Him. One of the very first Scripture verses that I learned by heart was a verse that just seemed to jump out at me from the very first time I read it. I was probably about eight when I read it in the book of Jeremiah. And I took God at His word when He said to me,

*"Call to me and I will answer you and tell you great and unsearchable things you do not know."*

Jeremiah 33:3

I believed that God had extended to me a personal invitation to ask Him questions and talk to Him. So I did. Especially when I was down at the river or on the shore of Lake Ontario, I would talk *and* listen to Jesus. I always felt better when I did. Sometimes we would just be quiet together.

I liked almost all of my time alone, but someone, usually Dad or My Oldest Brother, almost always entered my alone space and ripped away my peace. When we were in the years of building our *real* house on our property, I often opted out of working with Dad and My Brothers, choosing instead to keep things going in the trailer. There, during the work hours, I could be alone and peaceful. I preferred the quiet of doing the laundry, cooking, setting the table, cleaning up after and cleaning in general over the cacophony of chaos that played out in the construction zone with all the hammering, electric saws and drills, the tension of arguments and Dad's quick, harsh and crude criticisms about *"the shit-ass way sumbody done sumthin' wrong."*

One late afternoon when I was ten, and while everyone was working somewhere at something, I was finishing the dishes and putting a whole pile of silverware back in the drawer. I went deep inside my head. I felt safe enough to go there. I was wrong, once again.

With a handful of silverware still in my right hand, Dad was suddenly behind me, taking handfuls of me with both of his hands. Again. Grabbing and taking. He was all dirty and gross. Dad's hands with the long, black hairs and the stub of his trigger finger, were sweaty and grease-streaked. His work clothes were covered with sawdust and multi-colored stains from multiple sources. The brim of his weather-worn work hat hit me in the back of my head as he put his mouth on my shoulder. I wanted to take the forks and the knives and pierce them into his face and chest. But I couldn't move. I couldn't even scream. I could only hate. Dad just grabbed some more of me, pushing inside my panties and up under my shirt. Sliming up my body. Sliming up my mind. He suddenly stopped, pulled out, pulled away. *"Girl, git back to work. I was jus' playin' with ya. I jus' come in for a drink."*

Dad took a Coke from the fridge, ripped off its pull-tab, and tossing it into the garbage he took a long drink from the cold can. I heard the noise of his loud and thirsty swallows. He was as greedy with his drink as he was with his grabs. With one hand holding his Coke, Dad wiped his wet, dirty, hateful forehead on his wet, dirty, hateful sleeve, and walked out of the trailer and back to the work site.

I just stood frozen...still in front of the silverware drawer ...still with a handful of silverware in my right hand. My body couldn't move. I was stunned. I was shocked. I was sore. I went back deep inside my head, but it wasn't peaceful anymore, and my own voice shouted out at me, *"I am nothing. I mean nothing. I am not a person, not a girl, not anything. I am nothing. I am ripped at, grabbed at, hated and used. I hate Dad. I hate. I hate. I hate. I hate. I hate."*

*(There are times, even now, that whenever I am alone even if just for a moment, I go very quickly, almost instantaneously, deep inside myself...deep inside my head. That place for me now, as a grown woman, is most often very quiet, prayerful and peaceful. I go there very fast...and I go very far away from all that is happening around me. Tim has learned to gently call out my name – or make a lot of noise as he walks in the hall or comes up the stairs before entering a room where I am alone – even if he has just left me thirty seconds before. Without his gentle, or loud, arrival announcements, especially if approached from behind, I will still startle suddenly – usually with a little yelp, a quick drawing in of my breath and a self-protective move – as my peace in my alone-and-quiet-head-space is shattered.)*

Although the sting and the ugly power of this memory is gone, Dad's selfishness, cruelty and sick sexual abuse has forever changed what should be just a mundane and mindless activity for me – getting silverware out or putting silverware away. But I am not mindless when I approach the silverware drawer. The memory, though not its crippling effects, is still with me. With God's healing love and truth I have learned to take the courageous steps of reclaiming, continually, everything I am and everything I do, even if it's as mundane as getting out or putting away silverware. Evil had pervaded everything in my life...God, by His love, has claimed everything back.

My fierce independence, fueled by my desire to be alone and hidden and away from the hurt of my home, kept me on the move as often as possible. And sometimes my bike just wasn't fast enough or couldn't take me far enough. So by age ten, following in My Oldest Brother and My Big Brother's footsteps, I took to hitch-hiking into town as the fastest way to get away from home. By the time I was twelve, I felt very competent in the art of hitch-hiking. I was far too old-acting and old-thinking for my age. Growing up slowly – just being a child – was never an option for me.

One July night in 1972, I decided to go up to our town's Firemen's Field Days. And I planned to hitch-hike to get there. I just wanted to get away from the ugly and hurt of home for a little while. Going up to the Field Days gave me a legitimate excuse to be away. Everybody went up to the Field at some point during the weekend.

And that night, I just wanted to have a little bit of fun, maybe run into some people I knew. I knew a whole lot of the older kids, even some from the class of 1969 – who had graduated when I was only in fourth grade and many of whom were still living in town or, at least, hanging around town during Field Days. I had gotten to know these older kids, mostly older boys – young men, really – because they had helped out sporadically with the building of our house (which had been finished just the summer before) or they had worked at the frequently visited lumberyard or hardware store. As strange as it seems, I was always very at ease and comfortable with these older boys. Only from one of them did some stupid and crude joking come my way. I stayed away from him as much as possible whenever he came around our house or if I saw him in town. He just didn't seem safe to me. He and My Oldest Brother frequently hung around together – and exploits of drinking, getting high and getting laid were the topics most often heard from them. And I just didn't want to hear it. However, the other older boys were always good to me, treating me more like a friend than a little girl. Treating me like I was somebody who was cool to hang out with...cool to be around.

So that night, I wanted to go up to the Field Days to see if any of my older friends were hanging out. But the Field Days at night was not the best place for a younger girl to hang out. I should have gone up to the Field Days during the daytime to be part of the Kiddie Day Parade and the Decorated Bike Contest. I should have gone up to the Field Days during the special afternoon hours to take advantage of all the half-price rides on the Ferris Wheel, the Loop-de-Loop, the Tea Cups, the Swings, the Merry-Go-Round and every other crazy, spinning, circling, reduced fare ride offered to kids twelve and under.

But I didn't feel like or act like or look like a little girl of twelve. Physically, I had already reached my full, though not exactly soaring, height of five feet two inches tall by the time I was ten years old. The same year I started my period.

At twelve I felt very grown up, and I was stubbornly independent. I was going to the Field Days at night. That night. I walked down to the end of my driveway, with my back to our *real*, not-the-trailer house, and I listened, watched and waited for the first car to drive past my rural home. It wasn't too long, and my thumb was ready.

Down the road came a big, heavy-looking, dark blue car. I don't know what make or model it was. I never learned that stuff. I still can't distinguish most cars from any others except by referring to them by size and color. I know this is one thing about me that totally blows my tomboy image right out of the water. But cars, other than as a means to get some place, and quickly, just really aren't all that important to me.

As the big, heavy-looking, dark blue car came closer, I put my thumb out. Magic! The car stopped immediately right at the end of my driveway. This hitch-hiking thing was really working out for me. The Front Seat Passenger was even kind enough to reach behind himself to push open the back door so I could hop in easily. Two young mid-twenty-something men, who were currently living in the area to work on our farm-covered rural lands for the season, were my chauffeurs to the Field Days that night. They were heading up to the Field themselves for a little fun after a long, hard-working summer day in the black, rich soil on one of the local muck farms.

The ride to the Field was very comfortable. This car had an extra wide, ivory-colored back seat with lots of leg room – not all that necessary for my short legs. And the drive itself, though only a couple of miles in length, was actually kind of fun. I chatted it up quite a bit with these two young men. They both seemed so nice. They were very polite. As we arrived at the Field Days, The Front Seat Passenger got out quickly to open the back door for me.

As we all stood outside the car, I noticed for the first time that both The Driver and The Passenger were similarly dressed in clean, white tee shirts and new-looking, dark blue jeans. Their hair color and length were also similar – dark brown and falling long before landing just shy of their shoulders. Both had dark, coffee-black colored eyes. But there, the physical similarities ended – not extending to their builds or to their faces. These were very different.

The Driver was not exactly short, but he was not tall either. He was slim, yet honed in muscle as most young farm men are. His face was triangular and cratered with pockmarks. He seemed to have a little bit of a hard time making eye contact. The Driver hadn't been nearly as chatty as The Passenger – who had been much more comfortable conversing with me on the way into town.

The Passenger was taller than his friend, but still just a bit above medium height – not quite clearing six feet. His build was much more athletic with muscles reflective of the strenuous physical labor he used them for on a regular basis. His face was broad, blemish-free and welcoming with a wide-lipped, full-teeth smile.

*"Thanks for the ride. Good-bye."* I said to both The Driver and The Passenger as we parted ways.

I headed off to find a friendly face. The two young men headed off, like heat-seeking missiles, to the beer tent. They spent pretty much the whole night there. I spent mine wandering around talking with just about anyone who would talk to me and who would split the cost of sharing some of the fun and fabulous, summertime Field Days' food with me – hot dogs, hamburgers, hot sausages, rotisserie chicken, steamed clams, corn-on-the-cob, soda and, of course, cherry-flavored Sno-cones. Summertime food was at its absolute best at the Firemen's Field Days.

It seemed to get very late, very quickly. At about midnight I realized that the Field was really clearing out and there were fewer and fewer faces I recognized, and even fewer who had a car available to give me a ride back home. The two young farm workers who had picked me up at the end of my driveway were walking toward me. Their similarities in appearance were exaggerated by the brown bottles of beer they were each dangling in their right hands, by the fuzzy, blood-shot look in their eyes and the slight slur in their speech. Both smiled at me – that loose-lipped kind of smile people give when their mouths have been taken under control by the alcohol that has just passed through.

The Driver mumbled something that I couldn't understand. Either it was spoken incoherently or I wasn't supposed to understand. First looking at The Driver and then at me, The Passenger asked me in beer-soaked words, *"You wanna ride home?"*

I hesitated for just a second. Before I could say a word, The Passenger spoke again, *"It's OK. We know where you live. So? You wanna ride home? Or not?"*

As I was quickly weighing the offer of this much needed ride home against the experience I had with men and alcohol (and with men and boys even when they weren't drinking), another BLURSE of my personality kicked in even quicker, and I answered, *"Yes."*

BLURSE. *The Blessing*: I am a trusting person. In spite of everything I had gone through, I am still a trusting person. *The Curse:* I am a trusting person. In spite of everything I had gone through, I am still a trusting person...when I shouldn't be. BLURSE.

The three of us found their big, heavy-looking, dark blue car easily since it was one of only a dozen left in the parking field. The Driver slid into his seat behind the wheel. The Passenger again opened the car's back door for me. Only this time, his wide hand pushed on my back, just a little bit too hard, as I got into the wide, ivory-colored, leg-room-rich back seat. The door seemed to shut just a little bit too loudly behind me. The Passenger jumped into his assigned seat and slammed his door shut just a little bit too quickly.

The Driver turned the wrong way out of the parking field. We weren't going toward my home. We weren't going down my street. I tried to tell them which way to go. I tried to correct their mistake by dramatically pointing for them to go the other way. To turn around. Neither The Driver nor The Passenger responded to me. They weren't listening to me. They weren't seeing me. *I was mute. I was invisible. I was in danger.*

The car stopped. The lights and the engine were turned off. We were parked between the two huge buildings of a muck farm, on the edge of its vast field. The Driver got out and stood between the car and the farm buildings, blocking some of the beams from outside light that was mounted high on the taller of the two buildings. I watched him as he pulled on a light blue jean jacket to fend off the chill of the quickly cooling night air. The Driver turned his back and walked about fifteen feet away as The Passenger opened my door for the fourth time that night. Only it wasn't to let me out.

And it began. Pushing me over, but not too far, The Passenger brought his much wider, taller, stronger body next to mine. He slammed the door shut behind him and pushed down the locks on each of the four car doors with a quick jab from the side of his fist.

I didn't feel so grown up anymore. I felt four. I felt scared. I felt sick. I was absolutely helpless and I was so very little. I wanted to go home. Even to my home.

Waves of hands and fingers and tongue and mouth and lips and teeth and legs and penis crashed over me. Onto me. Into me. The Passenger attacked me and ripped into me, pushing under my clothing and into my body with a ferocity of violence and brutality that was beyond even the most outrageous assaults I had experienced from Dad and My Oldest Brother. I was bruised. I was bleeding. I was bit. I was devoured. I was destroyed. I was taken. I was gone.

I was crying. I was screaming. I was begging for it to *"Stop! Stop! Stop!"* But I had no power. I could not make it *"Stop!"*

The Passenger exploded and it finally stopped.

I was in such pain. I was so torn up. I was so beaten. My mind and my body seemed pulverized. I had no more strength. I had no more screams. The Passenger got out, and slipping on his pants as he stood at the open back car door, he called out to The Driver who was still at his watching post. I collapsed into a little, disjointed, semi-dressed, softly whimpering heap. Blood dribbled from my mouth, a few more drops came from a teeth-ripped wound on my right breast and landed on the ivory-colored seat to mix with the pool of slimy ooze from The Passenger's explosion.

The Driver approached the open back door and looked down at me as The Passenger pulled on his shirt. I thought the two of them were going to throw me into the black, wet soil of the muck where it would suck me down, swallow me, hide me. Finish me. Kill me. I was ready. Quietly ready. I was already dead.

I pulled myself up using the front seat as support and put one leg out the door to stand up (the leg that had my jeans and panties twisted and barely hanging on down at my ankle). The Passenger pushed my chest hard with his wide, strong hand so that I fell back onto the seat, my bottom landing in the pool of killing ooze and blood. Then scooping up my exited leg with both of his hands, The Passenger threw the rest of me back into the car. I was now more on the floor than on the seat. Both The Driver and The Passenger jumped in. The car's engine came to life. I wanted to die.

Taking a bonus, leftover swig from his beer bottle, The Passenger turned his head to look at me. *"Get your clothes on. And don't say nothing."* I got my clothes on and I said nothing. Not one word. I had done this before. I knew the drill.

The Passenger had told me the truth earlier that night when he said, *"We know where you live."* They did. They drove me back to my house. Barely pulling into the end of my driveway, The Driver stopped the car and The Passenger, for the final time that night, opened the big, heavy-looking, dark blue car's back door for me. And right there, in the same place where I had first been picked up by these men...by these monsters, The Passenger pulled me out of the car and tossed me out onto the end of my driveway.

It was about two or three in the morning when the car, The Driver and The Passenger sped off and away from me.

I forced my body into a standing position. Not fully, though. Hunching over holding my stomach and holding my chest was easier. There was just too much pain. I wiped a little more blood away from my mouth. And as I looked up I realized that the lights in the bedroom I shared with My Big Sister were on. Our room was on the second floor at the closest corner facing out onto the driveway and the street. The inside lights made it easy to see that it wasn't just My Big Sister who was awake and in our room. I could make out the silhouettes of the rest of my family.

I pushed through the pain. The cool air and the numbness of mind I felt helped to carry me along, even if it was slowly. I crawled up the stairs, almost on all fours, and used the hallway wall to hold me up as I walked down to my room. As I entered my bedroom doorway, six sets of eyes looked at me. I know they saw. I know they knew what must have happened to me. But no one came near.

The eyes of My Sister and My Brothers looked over to Mom and Dad for their signals...to know how they should act or respond. Mom spoke first, clapping her hands together, just once, as she said, *"Okay, kids. It's over. Sylane's home. Everybody go on out of here. It's time to get some sleep."* Dad echoed Mom's words, only harsher and louder, *"Go on now, git out! Y'all jus' go git settled down for the night. I don' wanna hear not one goddamn peep from y'all. I don' wanna hear not one word, not nothin' from y'all...at all! Y'all done heard me! Now git!"*

They obeyed. Even My Big Sister got out of our room. I moved deeper into my room as My Siblings moved out. Mom and Dad just looked at me. They knew. It was so obvious. My face and my body were bloodied and bruised. My hair and my clothing were all in twisted knots or torn in places. They knew.

After Mom and Dad rushed My Sister and My Brothers out of the room, they left too. Mom and Dad just walked out. Away from me. Away from my pain. And I was left alone.

Nobody helped to clean me up or comfort me. No one stayed to heal me or hug me. No one asked what had happened. No one stayed with me. I was just left alone.

I think Mom and Dad walked out on me because of another BLURSE of my personality that I already mentioned. *The Blessing:* I am a truth-teller. And telling the truth is good. *The Curse:* I am a truth-teller…in a family that did *not* want their own truths to be made known. BLURSE.

I think my parents were very afraid of the possibility that if they took me to the hospital or if they had me tell the police what had happened *that* night, that my BLURSE would take over and I wouldn't stop telling the truth…that I would not stop at just telling some health or law official about the truth of the rape of *that* night…but that I would go off on my own *Paul Harvey* version of: *"And now for the rest of the story"*…and tell the whole ugly, sickening truth about the horrendous abuse that takes place on other nights…on other days…right here in our home. Right here in my family.

I believe Mom and Dad chose to protect themselves *that* night from the possibility of our own ugly truth getting out. Mom and Dad chose to ignore me, my pain, my need, my life. And I was left all alone – a desperately hurting, angry and broken little twelve year old girl.

Yet even then, in that dark and ugly place in my head and my heart, I still knew, I still heard deep down, that I was not really left all alone. Not even for a moment. *Because God's grace and truth still speak in the darkest of places.*

My mind rushed me back to an earlier time…to a summer…to a week…to five long years before *that* night… and I knew that I wasn't left all alone.

I was seven. It was the summer of 1967, the summer we ended our two year sojourn in East Hartford, CT and moved back permanently to our small trailer in our small town in central New York. Dad was going to be having one of his yet-to-come numerous surgeries. And with all the logistics and details for the moving transition and Dad's medical care, Mom and Dad needed to find a way to keep us five kids out of the way (get rid of us) for at least one week of that crazy summer. Grandma and Grandpa or babysitters could be available to help most of the rest of the time.

And for that one week five years before *that* night, Mom and Dad had found a summer camp to send all five of us children…all at the very same time. The type of camp didn't matter to Mom and Dad. They just desperately needed to have all five of us children out of the house for that one week. *(Let's be fair. Even the most loving of parents in the most loving of homes should be entitled to have at least one week each year away from their five children who were all-born-within-less-than-five-years-of-each-other!)* So, no, the type of camp didn't matter to Mom and Dad.

But it mattered very much to God!

So, for just one short week during the summer of 1967, My Big Sister, My Oldest Brother, My Big Brother, My Little Brother and I were sent to OBC – Ontario Bible Camp. A Christian camp. OBC – where their Welcome Sign reads, and their volunteer staff is committed to: *"Teaching and Preaching God's Word."*

It was there at OBC, on the shore of my beloved Lake Ontario, that God interrupted and intervened in my life for the first time (that I was aware of it, anyway). And it was there at OBC that God first, and for all eternity, intertwined His Spirit and His Word into my heart, my head and my soul. And God did it by loving me…calling me into His eternal salvation and into an intimate, powerful relationship offered through His Son, my Savior Jesus Christ.

Each evening at OBC we would all gather, staff and campers together, into the chapel – a big barn-like, open building – for a worship time of singing and listening to the Camp Pastor teach us something from God's Word…from the Bible.

I liked those evening services. They were warm and happy. The songs were good and fun to clap and dance to with everybody joining together. I always did like to sing and clap and dance. And here I could. And here each night at OBC, even during just the short breaks between songs or as I lay down my head to sleep in my own bed, in my roomy cabin, I could hear the sound of crickets and other night bugs making their clicking-clacking and humming sounds. Here I was warm and happy. Here I was safe.

One evening at our chapel worship service, the Camp Pastor did his *Teaching and Preaching of God's Word* from John 3:16:

> ***"For God so loved the world that***
> ***he gave his one and only Son, that whoever believes in***
> ***him shall not perish but have eternal life."***

John 3:16

It seemed as if that Pastor-man was speaking directly to me. I can still see his big brown eyes looking right into mine. His eyes were filled with so much love. So much truth. He was so happy to be telling us about God's love for us, about the salvation of Jesus that God offers to us. It was as if God was reaching out with all of His heart, with all of His love and with all of His power right to me…right there in my seat in the Chapel at OBC. And even though I know My Big Sister, My Oldest Brother, My Big Brother, My

Little Brother and all the other Camp Staff and Camp Kids were sitting right there with me in the Chapel that evening, I sensed that I was being spoken to very personally…that God was intimately and clearly speaking right to me through the voice and the words of that Pastor-man who was *Teaching and Preaching God's Word.*

That Pastor-man with his big brown eyes explained the amazing love of our God that was expressed in John 3:16. He explained that God not only loves me – *has* love for me – but that God *is* Love. And that God, who *is* Love, is so great that He sent His precious Son Jesus to die for me…to die for the forgiveness of my sins…to die for the forgiveness of all the sins of everyone who believes and trusts in Him.

And that Pastor-man explained that our God is also Holy and Perfect. And we can *only* come to God, fully and forever, if we also are holy and perfect and without sin.

Oh, my gosh! Even as a seven year old little girl, I knew I wasn't sinless. I wasn't pure or perfect. I could be so mean and so ugly, so selfish, so angry and so jealous at times. I lied. I hated. And I realized that I needed Jesus to forgive me. *(And now, nearly a half century later, I am ever more deeply convinced that I need Jesus…that every single one of us needs Jesus.)*

*"For God so loved the world that he gave his one and only Son, that whoever believes in him shall not perish but have eternal life."*
John 3:16

And that loving, happy-to-tell-us, brown-eyed Pastor-man clearly explained to me, and to all of us in the chapel that night, what I came to believe right then…and what I continually come to understand more and more deeply with each passing year: God *did* give His one and only Son to the world. It was out of His love that our Holy God chose to *give* Jesus, His Sinless Son, *over to death* for the forgiveness of my sin...for the forgiveness of each and every sin ever committed, or yet to be committed, by each and every person to ever live in this world.

I need Jesus! And so does everyone. Jesus, God's Holy Son had to die in my place. Jesus had to die for all of us.

Jesus is the only way for any of us to come entirely and for all eternity into the presence of the Sovereign God, our Heavenly Father. We cannot do or give anything to earn the salvation that Jesus offers to us freely. We can never be good enough through anything we choose to do...or be good enough because of the things we choose not to do. We cannot do enough of even the kindest deeds to counter-balance, or somehow make up for, anything we have done that has gone against the loving holiness of our God. We can never, even through the most beautiful or rigorous of spiritual disciplines – such as prayer, meditation, fasting, Bible study, tithing, selfless acts of service – save ourselves from the power that sin and death has over our lives. We cannot make our own way – no matter how hard we try or how much we want it – into the full loving, saving, freeing, transforming eternal-life-giving presence of our Holy, Almighty God.

But God is able to bring us fully and forever to Himself. And God has already made our way to Him through the sacrificial death of Jesus Christ.

Our response must be, and can only be, to humbly cry out to our God and accept His perfect and sufficient way for our salvation – a salvation that cannot be obtained or added to by anything we desire or do. Our salvation is

God's free love gift to us that came through the death of God's pure and perfect Son Jesus. His death on the cross, His blood that was spilled, is the only acceptable sacrifice to God through which our sins are forgiven fully and forever.

And as God's perfect sacrifice to pay the death penalty for our sins, Jesus Christ did not stay dead! Jesus is the Living Lord! Our faithful and just God, in His love and through His unlimited power, raised Jesus Christ to life for all eternity! Through Jesus, our Heavenly Father has lovingly and irrevocably promised that we, too, will be resurrected from the dead...*that we shall not perish but have eternal life*...eternal life with our God.

It is only when we humbly respond to God's call – when we agree with God – when we accept God's way, God's gift of salvation and eternal life through Jesus Christ that we are brought fully and forever into an unending, inseparable relationship with our God who loves us so much!

And that night at OBC on the shore of Lake Ontario, that Pastor-man was the voice and heart of God as he explained God's way for salvation and the intimate and forever relationship I could have with my Heavenly Father.

But that Pastor-man didn't stop at just the explanation of God's love shown to us through the sacrificial death of His Son Jesus. Oh, no. Just hearing this eternal truth isn't enough. That Pastor-man, with his big brown eyes so filled with love, asked me...asked each of us in the Chapel that night, very clearly, *"Do you believe it?"*

A decision had to be made. An action had to be taken.

I raised my little seven year old hand and I said, *"YES! I believe!"* And I know that right then and there Jesus became my Savior that very night in the Chapel at OBC on the shore of Lake Ontario. The blood of Jesus shed on the cross was my only way to be forgiven and made right with God. And I knew *that* night that I had been given eternal life and an eternal love relationship with my God!

At the end of *that* way-too-short week at OBC, I had to go home. Mom pulled up in our big, black station wagon with three seats, the farthest one facing out the back window. We had to pack up. We had to go home.

I didn't want to go home. I didn't want to leave this place right on the shore of Lake Ontario. I didn't want to leave my single bed where I got to sleep alone. Where there was never a danger zone. I didn't want to leave the singing and the clapping and the dancing to go where there were too many ugly words, too much anger, too much screaming and too many gun shots. I didn't want to leave this place where my very nice and funny camp counselor had taught me how to wrap my long, beautiful hair up into a towel-turban. And I definitely didn't want to leave this place where the *Teaching and Preaching of God's Word*, through the faithfulness of all the Camp Staff and, especially, through the voice and heart of that brown-eyed Pastor-man, had changed my life forever. Before I left OBC, I was given a Bible of my very own...for the learning and believing of God's Word.

*(I think the camp staff at OBC may have wondered over the years what could have possibly made those two very deep, very long ruts in the camp's dirt driveway. On my first trip back to OBC, forty-two years after that life-changing week – when I was invited to facilitate a portion of the counselor training: Leading a Child to Christ, and, then, speak in the chapel at the Commissioning Service of*

*Counselors and Staff for their Summer Ministry 2009 – I finally explained the long-time mystery of those two very deep, very long ruts: They were made by my two little, seven year old, dragging, fighting feet that didn't want to go home.)*

But I did go home. I got myself and the big cloth bag I had used for a suitcase into our big, black station wagon where Mom, My Big Sister, My Oldest Brother, My Big Brother and My Little Brother were all waiting for me. I sat way in the back where the seat faced out the rear window. I wanted to look at the Lake and at OBC for as long as I possibly could. They got smaller and smaller and, then, disappeared from my sight way too soon.

And way too soon, I was back to my life at home that was still, and for many years after, locked in the hell of ugly and evil abuse and incest. I wished OBC was my real home. I wished I could always feel warm and happy, safe and loved. But that wasn't my reality. Not then.

Yet deep down inside of me, inside my heart where Jesus now lived, I knew, even at seven years old, that my eternal life was now held in the hands of my loving God – regardless of what the hands of others did to me.

I knew then that Jesus loved me and would never leave me alone. Not even for a moment.

And *that* night, five long years later when I was twelve, *that* night after being viciously, brutally, sexually attacked by The Passenger...after The Driver stood guard at his watching post...after Mom and Dad had left me and just walked out and away from me...even then, I knew that Jesus loved me and would never leave me alone. Not even for a moment. *Because God's grace and truth still speak in the darkest of places.*

But that knowledge that God was with me did *not* calm the fury or the hate raging inside of me. That knowledge did not heal the pain in every part of my twelve year old body. That knowledge did not lift the gut-wrenching anguish that crushed and tortured every thought in my mind, every portion of my soul.

But that knowledge that God was with me *did* move me to call out to Him. But when I called out, it was not the sweet, thankful, faith-filled prayer I had prayed at seven years old when I accepted Jesus as my Savior and the gift of my eternal relationship with God.

No! God wasn't so lucky this time. I was crazed, absolutely, outrageously crazed. And I screamed out to God. I screamed *at* God with every ounce of the overwhelming anguish and anger that was taking over my head, my body and my soul…taking over me.

*"God, I am twelve years old and I feel like I'm ninety! I should be playing with Barbies! Not going through this! Not living this hell! God, You had better do something about this or I will kill myself! I'll give You a little bit of time, God! But You had better do something about this, and do it quick, God! OR-I-WILL-KILL-MYSELF!"*

I wanted to die. There was nothing to live for anymore. My world, my entire world, my entire self had been used up, ripped away from me and barred from any safety anywhere. I could not control the way others hurt me. I could not control the way others killed me.

So, I determined in the reason-consuming rage and the life-twisting anguish of my soul, to take control. I would do the killing myself. Of myself. In my way.

# 7

***In my anguish I cried to the LORD,
and He answered me
by setting me free.***
*Psalm 118:5*

That night when I screamed out, screamed *at* God, I was in absolute, unrelenting anguish. Anguish of mind, body and soul. I had had enough. My plan was to kill myself. And I knew I could do it…because of another BLURSE of my personality that had reared its ugly head.

*The Blessing*: I am a woman of determination, perseverance and commitment. When I say that I'm going to do something or get something done or when I commit myself to a task, I take it very seriously. I will do everything in my power that I possibly can in order to get the task done and carry through with the promise, with the commitment, I have made. *The Curse:* I can be one of the most stubborn, willful, strong-minded, pigheaded people you would ever want to meet. BLURSE.

And so, on that July night, I wrote a suicide note. I had resolutely formed my plan. And I would be stubbornly true to my word. I would give God *a little bit* of time…but God had better *do something...and do it quick*…or my plan for killing myself would go into effect. I had absolutely no doubt – and I had absolutely no fear at all – about fulfilling my plan to take my life. Death had to be better than this.

God had a plan too. And God had already written His living and active, purpose-achieving Word for me and for my life. And it was *freedom.*

The morning after the rape no one woke me up. No one disturbed me. It was Sunday and the house was pretty quiet. I went into the bathroom and for the first time since getting home, I really looked at myself in the mirror. I didn't feel anything. I didn't think anything. I just looked.

I got into the shower and began washing off The Passenger. Washing off the latest filth to overtake me. All of me hurt. All of me felt foreign and misshapen, bruised and dirty. My own touch hurt me. The water ran on. No one banged on the door with the usual warning, *"Don't use up all the hot water! You're not the only one living here, you know!"* I shampooed my hair three times. I washed my body four times. I wished I was already dead countless times.

Tears mixed with the shower water running down my face. But I hadn't invited these tears, and I wasn't about to give into them or give them any power. I stayed cold to my own heart. And I turned the water on even hotter. It didn't matter anymore. Nothing did.

I dressed and came down the hallway to the living room. The TV was going, but not too loudly. Dad was reading a section from the big Sunday Newspaper, *The Syracuse Herald American.* His Pall Mall cigarette was sitting in the corner of his mouth, his coffee cup on a TV tray next to his recliner. Dad looked over his paper at me, nodded and greeted me with, *"Girl..."* (kind of a pre-curser to the multi-purpose *"Dude...")*. My Big Sister was sitting on the couch reading *Parade Magazine*, one of *The Herald's* many Sunday sections. Softly from My Big Sister came, *"Hey, Laney..."*

I nodded and mouthed, *"Morning,"* to both, and repeated it when I entered the kitchen where Mom was sitting at the table with her coffee, cigarette and preferred section of *The Herald*.

Mom looked at me, all up and down. Apparently nothing caused her any overt alarm, so she asked, *"Are you hungry?"*

*"Yes. I'll just get myself some cereal."* I got my *Rice Krispies* with an overload of sugar and some cold milk and sat down at the table with Mom. We didn't talk. But it wasn't uncomfortable. It was just quiet. *The Funnies* (as we called the comic strip section) were easily within my reach. It was a good distraction. So were Snap, Crackle and Pop.

It was mid-morning and all three of My Brothers seemed to be gone. There was one great benefit of it being summer and now living in a bigger-than-the-trailer house. We all had more space especially when the weather was good. We didn't have to be so crowded together.

I decided I needed to be gone too. After breakfast I got on my bike and started riding and I just kept on riding. I did the same thing the next day and the next day and the next. Years later when I saw the 1994 movie *Forrest Gump*, I totally understood and connected with Forrest and his need to just go and keep on going. He ran. I rode.

And on as many days as I could, I would get up in the morning and ride my bike like a maniac. I just had to ride. I just had to be gone. But my suicide note was not gone. It was always with me. My suicide plan was just as determined. Just as present.

I didn't talk to God a whole lot the rest of that summer. But on those few days when I did go down to my favorite, Big Rock at the river, I *would* let Jesus sit with me. But I usually had my back to Him. He never seemed to mind that I wasn't talking or listening to Him. I wasn't screaming at Him anymore either. I was just quiet.

The summer passed. The first day of eighth grade arrived. *"God...? Are You going to do something? Quick?"* I was not any less certain about my plan to kill myself or my ability to carry out my plan. My suicide note was still in my pocket. But a little bit of excitement about the change that a new school year brings had crept in – uninvited, but it had still crept in.

So, with My Sister and My Brothers, I walked out to the end of my driveway to wait for Bus number 52, the bus that had always been our school bus. And *right there* at the end of my driveway – where just two months before I had been thrown down by The Passenger – God's plan of freedom for me, at least the beginning of it, showed up. Actually, drove up and stopped to let me in.

Because God is true to His Word.

> **In my anguish I cried to the LORD,**
> **and He answered me by setting me free.**
> Psalm 118:5

A school bus did pull up, but it wasn't Bus number 52. I got on anyway. And on this Bus-*not-number*-52, was a girl named Becky with a big, friendly, smiley face and lots to talk about. And we did. We talked all the way to school. By the time we unloaded by the row of glass doors in the back of the high school (which all the seventh through twelfth graders in our district attended), we were best buds. Oh! I could hardly wait for the bus ride after school with Becky!

On the way home on Bus-*not-number*-52, Becky and I could not chat fast enough to tell each other all about our first day of this new school year. Besides the fact that Bus-*not-number*-52 had different kids on it, I noticed that our rural bus route seemed even longer and more windy than usual. I didn't mind. I was with Becky.

We came to Becky's house, she got off. And the bus continued on its country road path. A full forty-five minutes later I was still on the bus (that was okay by me, it meant less time at home) when we passed right in front of Becky's house again. *Hmmmmm?*

The next day on our bus ride into school, Becky and I came up with a brilliant plan. And we put it right into action on the bus ride back home from school! We asked (actually, we begged, pleaded, cajoled and annoyed) Mr. Bus Driver to please, let me get off at Becky's house for those forty-five minutes the first time he drove by there. I promised to be ready to get right back on the bus as soon as he came by the second time. I told Mr. Bus Driver that he didn't even have to come to a full stop…he only had to just slow down enough…open the doors…and I would jump right back on the bus! *"Please, pleeeeease, Mr. Bus Driver, please let me get off at Becky's for those forty-five minutes!"*

I think Mr. Bus Driver finally agreed with our plan just to shut us up! We wore him down through our overly-enthusiastic-and-annoying-junior-high-school-girl-begging.

Our plan had come to pass. On the bus ride back home after the second day of school, I got off at Becky's house. We walked together up her farmer-driveway, chatting and laughing all the way. Her big, white farmhouse was up on our left, and her family's big, red barn – with its wide doors slid open and several cow bums plainly visible – was up at the end of the driveway. And as we walked up, Becky's farmer-dad, Mr. D., all dressed in his farmer-blue-jean-overalls, was walking down.

I watched Becky and her dad as they, first, smiled and waved to each other while still a bit of a distance apart. This seemed so strange to me. But I liked it. There was such a natural sweetness and warmth in the way Becky and Mr. D. looked at each other.

Then, as we met in the middle of their driveway, I took a step back as Mr. D. welcomed his Becky back home with a big, loving Daddy-hug. I just stood there and watched. I couldn't even begin to get my mind fully around what I was seeing. My heart and my spirit knew something far deeper than my mind could grasp at that moment...far deeper than could possibly be expressed in words right then.

Mr. D's love for Becky was so protective and good, so strong and safe. It was so pure. There was nothing ugly or taking. There was nothing twisted or sexual in Mr. D.'s Daddy-hug that he gave Becky. I saw the loving, caring, joyful, pure love of a Daddy-man for his precious daughter. I knew I was watching the love that a Daddy-man is *supposed* to have for his little girl...for his baby...for his child.

That day in that driveway, I *saw* a glimpse of God's good love for His children right before my eyes. A love that is pure and real. A love that protects and builds up. And I liked it. And I wanted it.

And when Becky's dad got done hugging her, he hugged *me*.

For the first time in my life, I *felt* the pure touch of a Daddy-man for myself. Through Mr. D., I started to understand the heart of my Heavenly Father that was so completely different from the heart of my earthly father.

*(It would still be many years before I could call God "Father." God had a great deal to reconfigure and heal in my mind for that to happen. And God's good, unfailing love is able – was able – to do just that. "Father," and more intimately and more often, "Abba" are the names I use when listening and talking to my God, the Sovereign Lord of all creation...who loves me so very much.)*

Becky and I went on into the house. Mr. D. went back to the cows. Mrs. D. and Becky's Grandma were in the kitchen when we came in. They were both funny, chatty, a little short, a little round and very smiley. And both gave big, good hugs to me too.

Becky's family had a lot of love to share. And food always came with it. One of our usual (unusual) after school snacks was tuna fish sandwiches with chocolate milk fresh from their cows. (Well, actually, we did have to add the chocolate syrup to the milk!) *I still love that culinary combination. It was comfort food to my body and my soul. Just as being with Becky and her family was for me.*

Becky, Mr. and Mrs. D. and Grandma all loved on me. They loved on me with kindness and welcome, warmth, humor and food. They loved on me with their time and attention. Becky's family was not perfect. They were real, with real problems. But they really loved each other. And they really loved Jesus. And because they did, they really loved me.

You darn well better believe that I got off that Bus-*not-number*-52 at Becky's house every day after school that I possibly could for every one of those fun and fabulous forty-five minutes!

Becky's family received me into their home, into their lives, into their family. They were the very arms of God reaching out to hug me, to hold me, to comfort me...to receive me. God used Becky and her family to open the truth of God's healing love for me in a very intimate way.

> *Though my father and mother forsake me,*
> *the LORD will receive me.*

Psalm 27:10

God's arms also brought me into this family so that I would be brought to Church, Sunday School and Youth Group. Brought to the places and the people who would help me grow in my (up until that point, a very much on-my-own) faith and understanding of God's Word.

During those five years, from the summer I had believed in Jesus as my Savior at OBC through to the summer I was raped by The Passenger, almost the entirety of my faith growth was done alone as God spoke to me through the Bible and through His Spirit – as Jesus talked with me at the river.

I had been given a bit of help over the years when in third grade through sixth grade I had asked Mom if I could be signed up for *Religious Ed*. Nice Ladies met with us on certain Wednesdays for about an hour. They told us the *Big Bible Stories*: Creation, Adam and Eve, Noah, Abraham, Isaac, Jacob, Joseph, Moses, and lots about Jesus – His miracles of healing and feeding thousands, and so many at the water: Jesus' baptism, a big catch of fish, calming the storm, walking on water, the woman at the well and, of course, we were told the story of Jesus' death and resurrection for our salvation. And all these *Big Bible Stories* were illustrated by the Nice Ladies on *their big flannel board.* I had never seen stories told that way before. I thought it was cool. And sometimes the Nice Ladies would let us kids put the flannel pieces on their flannel board. I liked the way they felt. I liked hearing their stories.

Later on those days when I got home from school, I would go check out their stories for myself in the Bible I had been given at OBC. Yep, they were all in there.

But now God was working out His *freedom* plan for me in an intense and stepped-up sort of way. A huge part of that was through Becky and her family getting me involved in Youth Group. Within a short period of time from when I joined my first Youth Group, there was a change in the adult leadership. A new couple, Raylene and Jack, came to lead the Youth Group at our church. They were pretty young. And pretty cool. And they loved Jesus. They loved the Bible. And they had so much love and passion and enormous patience for us junior high and senior high school kids.

When Raylene and Jack said the name *Jesus Christ*, it was in a way far different than I had ever heard it said by Dad or Mom or Grandpa. When Raylene and Jack said *Jesus*, it was hearing them speak the name of their very best friend, who was also their Holy Lord and their Mighty Savior. Raylene and Jack made known to me (and all of us who would *let* it be known to us) the very real and deeply intimate love God has for each person. Raylene and Jack helped us to know the living, transforming grace and truth of God's Word and the powerful presence of the Holy

Spirit that Jesus Himself had promised would come upon *and* live in His followers.

God was coming at me from so many angles. God was opening up relationships with so many people who were not just going through the motions of religiosity, but who sincerely wanted to live out their faith relationship with Jesus in authentic, every day-to-day ways.

And God stirred my heart to want to live. Really live. To live in spite of the deathblows of the evil and ugly abuse still going on at home...to live still knowing that the possibility of pain and attack from a stranger or a friend or a circumstance could come into my life at any time...in any place...in any form...from anyone.

Jesus Christ had already given His life for me for all eternity. And Jesus called me to trust Him with all of my life on this side of Heaven – as hellish as that could be and already had been. Jesus called me to trust Him and His love for me. To trust Him with all that I am at every moment of every day in every circumstance.

> *Trust in the LORD with all your heart,*
> *and lean not on your own understanding;*
> *in all your ways acknowledge God,*
> *and he will direct your paths.*
> Proverbs 3:5-6

It was time to rip up the suicide note. It was time to live.

It was time to acknowledge what God had been doing in my life: God had answered, and was answering my prayer of anguish, and through God's unrelenting love and the love of other followers of Jesus Christ, God was setting me *free*.

And there was music. Lots of music. The Christian singing group, *Celebrate Life*, made up almost entirely of teens from around the Horseheads, NY area, came to our church to give a concert and to tell of their faith in Jesus. I had no idea that groups like this existed. I got especially close, and stayed close for a number of years, with a few of those fabulous, fun, faithful – singing and clapping and dancing – teens.

And there was Tim Mack. Playing his guitar and singing in his deep, strong bass voice *(my very favorite sound in the world...Tim's voice still takes my breath away and warms my heart)* at Raylene and Jack's apartment during our weekly Youth Group meetings.

Although I had known Tim as a friend of My Big Brother since he was about six and I was about five years old, we had never had any real contact with each other. But there Tim was. With his beautiful voice, big brown-green eyes, thick, curly auburn-red hair and a smile that made everyone around him want to smile.

There Tim was. Right there *with* me in this truth-telling, life-changing, Jesus-honoring Youth Group. Tim was there *for* me...and I was there *for* Tim. First, as brother and sister in Christ in our Youth Group – enjoying the fun, the depth, the activities and getting to know and be filled with God's passionate desire to make us passionate for Him. (And Tim and I tended to make Jack a little crazy from time to time since we would rather talk to each other than fully listen to him. Oh, teens!)

Within the next couple of years, Tim and I became very best friends. Then, in my junior year and Tim's senior year of high school, on November 9, 1975 to be exact, (and less than six months after I had told Mom, in my pre-surgery, drug-induced state, that I wanted a Big Mack) Timmy and I had our very first date. We went to see the musical

*Godspell* in Syracuse with a group of friends, and I was the last to be taken home…but Timmy didn't take me right home. This was no ordinary November 9 in central New York. The weather was more like a late summer evening, unusually mild and warm. No coats required. And we just didn't want this magical time to end. So, before taking me home, Tim and I went, first, to the elementary school playground to swing on the swings, slide down the slide and spin around on the merry-go-round. It was still too beautiful to go home, so we drove to the shore of Lake Ontario…to walk and talk and, *yes*, kiss. It was so clear to both of us, even as crazy young as we were, that we loved each other and believed that God had brought us together by His good love and plan. Tim and I were married on June 7, 1980. So, I'm thinking we were probably right.

God has used Tim *with* and *for* me (and I know God has used me *with* and *for* Tim) over and over again…over all of our years together…to continue and further the loving, transforming work of God's fullest *freedom* for my life.

But during that first year of our Youth Group time with Raylene and Jack, it was Raylene who God used in a mighty and direct way to point me to God's *second* greatest freedom for my life. God's *first* greatest freedom – *salvation* – I had received at age seven when I believed and accepted that Jesus, God's One and Only Son, had died for my sins and rose from the dead to give me eternal life.

But God knew that being saved by His love wasn't enough. He had so much more in mind for me. As God does for all of His children. God had *transformation* and His full and powerful, healing freedom in mind for me. God continued to actively answer my twelve year old prayer of brokenness and anguish in ways that I could not ever have imagined or even understood. God had undeniable, invincible *transformation* in mind to bring me His true, healing freedom – His powerful, life-changing *love* to my spirit, my heart, my mind and my soul.

And one night, God brought His *second* greatest freedom to me in a corner in Raylene and Jack's apartment.

I loved Raylene and she loved me. I felt so comfortable with her and would often go hang out at her apartment after school or stay there, extra long and late, well after our Youth Group meetings had ended. *(God bless all youth workers!)* God had given Raylene a deep gift of insight and compassion for all of us kids. And, even though I had never talked about the ugliness and abuse happening in my family, Raylene recognized that something in me was very broken and hurting.

I was thirteen by this time and, not unlike many girls my age, I suffered from some of the expected, hormonally-induced, temporary insanity that often came with being an adolescent. My emotions were all over the place. I would be chatty and outgoing one moment...then completely withdrawn and lost in my own little head the next. I would be goofy, silly, laughing, singing and dancing one moment...then so sad, lonely, crying and feeling completely rejected and unwanted the next.

None of this was all that terribly unusual for a lot of my peers. But Raylene recognized that in me, even as a very over-sensitive teenage girl, this roller-coaster of emotions was spinning me out of control and had come from some place other than just my hormonal glands.

Out of love for me, and I believe out of sheer obedience to our God, one night after all the other kids had left from our Youth Group meeting to go home, Raylene came over to me – over to the corner of her apartment where I was standing. And with her glasses slipping down her nose a bit like they always did, Raylene looked at me over the top of them with her big dark eyes. There was a lot of love in those eyes. But they were also filled with determination and strength. Raylene placed her two hands on my shoulders and said, *"Sylane, you have got to tell somebody what is hurting you so badly."*

I just looked at her a bit surprised. She was so direct. But still so tender. And she was blocking my only path to escape out of the corner. But my heart didn't really want to leave. I just shrugged my shoulders against Raylene's hands. I didn't answer. I just looked at her. Her eyes were brimming with tears. Tears that belonged to me.

Raylene's hold on my shoulders was warm and strong and demanding, *"Sylane, what is hurting you so badly? You have got to tell somebody."*

But the voice that came wasn't mine. And it wasn't speaking to Raylene. It was the voice of my Dad and Mom, My Oldest Brother. It was the voice of The Passenger. And even though it was screaming loudly and viciously and pointing its sharp, condemning, threatening finger at me, only I heard the voice…only I felt the cruel and dangerous threat. It was the same voice and threat that I had known from the very first time Dad raped me. It was the voice and threat that had too often been repeated. Too often shamed me. Too often scared me. It had power. I had none.

*Don't you tell anyone! Don't you make a goddamn peep! Keep your goddamn mouth shut! Don't say nothing! Don't you tell anyone!*

And up to that day, I never did. I had never told anyone. The voice and the threat it made by its cruelly, intimidating power had held me locked in my hell with my mouth tightly shut.

But there was Raylene, standing in front of me, holding my shoulders, filled with the love of Jesus. And asking me to tell her what was hurting me so badly.

*Love unlocks hell.* And for the next three hours I told.

I told Raylene of the screaming and the hitting, of the belts and the knives. Of Tanya. Of the guns. Of the fear. Of the running and the hiding. And although the voice and the threat kept coming at me, trying to shut me down and shut me up, God's love flowing through Raylene was coming at me even stronger, even more fiercely than the evil. God's love was fighting to keep me talking. And I did. And I told of Dad's touching. Of Dad's raping. Of Dad's taking and grabbing and sliming and destroying. Of Mom's watching. Of Mom's silence. Of Mom's rejection. Of the sickness and brutality that came from My Oldest Brother...that he had learned dangerously, frighteningly well. Of the sickness and twistedness in all of our relationships. I told of The Driver and The Passenger. I told of my plan to kill myself.

And I cried, and I sobbed, and I screamed and I swore. Snot poured out from my nose, covering my face more quickly than I could wipe it off on my sleeve. I shook. And I shook my fists. I stomped my feet. I slapped and banged my hands against that corner wall.

I didn't just tell Raylene *what was hurting me so badly.* I spewed out and emotionally vomited all over her so much of the poison from all the hateful, evil, ugly, filthy, cruel things that had been done to me.

But I didn't stop there.

Raylene and God had unlocked my hell. And all hell was coming out. Ferociously. And with a vengeance. I told and I screamed out all of the hate and anger I felt for my family and for everyone who had ever hurt me. I hated them all with a viciousness and a passion that I had never even known I had inside of me. Or had ever admitted was there. I could feel the face and force of hate take over my own face...take over my eyes, my mind, my body, my all.

*I hate them. I hate them. I hate them. I hate them. I hate them. I hate them.*

Through all of this time, through all of my unleashed regurgitation of all these evils that had been inflicted on me and through all of my crazed rantings of my absolute hate for all my offenders, Raylene just stood there. Listening. Loving. She hated the evil. I could see that in her eyes that brimmed with those tears that belonged to me.

After these three hours, Raylene stood there calm and strong. I was completely spent, completely ripped open, completely exhausted emotionally, mentally, physically, spiritually. My head hurt. My throat hurt. My hands hurt. My stomach hurt. Even my bones hurt.

*What now? I've opened up something I can't take back. Something I can't do anything about.*

I was so tired. I was so done. I just wanted to slump down, curl up in that corner and fall asleep. Forever.

But that wasn't God's plan for my freedom.

Raylene took my shoulders one more time. And I now realize that God must have been holding onto Raylene far tighter, holding her by His powerful love...and holding her to complete obedience to His truth. Because Raylene then offered me God's *second* greatest act of freedom for my life. I just didn't recognize it immediately.

Raylene took her hands off my shoulders, leaving to God the job of holding me there in that corner now.

Looking right into my eyes, looking deep into my soul with all the poison and rips from the hateful things done to me and all the arsenal of the hate I was filled with, Raylene stood there and quietly, unflinchingly spoke three words, *"Now you forgive."*

I was totally shocked. Dumbfounded. Blind-sided. Angry. Confused. Hurt. I just stared at Raylene. Every natural instinct within me was screaming out with a burning force and an even hotter indignation, *"NO!"*

I didn't say a word out loud. I couldn't. But inside, my head was whirling and shouting at me. *I had finally told someone about all of the ugly and the evil and the sick and the cruel and horrific and the frightening things I had gone through...was still going through...in my own home...in my own town! I had finally told someone! And this! This is what I get in return! 'Now you forgive?!' What kind of answer is that! I finally let out the hate that I feel! The hate that I have absolutely every right in the world to feel! Everything I just told her is so hateful! So bizarre and cruel! How can this be the response I get? 'Now you forgive?!' What is she thinking? What is she talking about? What is she doing? Didn't she hear anything I said? Doesn't she care anything about me? Doesn't she care at all about all that I have gone through?*

Raylene quietly, unflinchingly spoke *those* three words again, *"Now you forgive."*

More staring on my part. *All I had been living through, all I had suffered, all of my hurt and anger and hate were just being totally ignored. I was being ignored. Again. What is she doing to me? Why is she doing this to me?! I thought she loved me.* Again, inside my head I fiercely, stubbornly screamed, *"NO!"*

But it wasn't *Raylene* who was doing anything to me. And, *yes,* she did love me. Raylene loved me enough to push through all of her own human feelings that would want to somehow rescue me in her own strength and to offer me her own sense of healing.

Raylene loved me enough to obey God's word and way to offer me God's *true* healing…and beyond that…to offer me God's *true* freedom. The battle here was for my mind, my heart, my deepest inner healing, my ultimate freedom. The battle here was for my very life. And Raylene was being held tightly in God's love and strength that was far beyond anything she could possibly have offered me in her own love and strength. Only in obedience to God could Raylene offer me more than transient pity. Only in obedience to God could Raylene offer me God's way to a powerful transformation.

God's word and way came at me again. Calmly, truthfully, persistently, powerfully. Raylene repeated a third time, *"Now you forgive."*

There it was. In that moment I recognized that *this* was God's bizarre, passionate, absolutely counter-intuitive way of answering my anguished prayer for God to *"do something about"* – something amazing and life-changing – about my pain, about my hurt and my hate.

In that moment I recognized that *this forgiveness* towards all who had hurt me so horribly was a *gift* from God. *This forgiveness* was not something that I could have mustered up from my own human determination. I did not have some kind of extra dose of maturity or goodness deep within my character that could offer *this forgiveness.* This kind of life-transforming, true and healing, freedom-bringing *forgiveness* is a complete *gift* from God alone.

And in that moment that's exactly how I saw *this forgiveness.* It was almost as if God was handing me – in that moment, in that corner of Raylene and Jack's apartment – a tangible, enormous gift. *This forgiveness…* the very ability to *forgive now…*was a gift from God.

I could not possibly *buck up* enough or be strong enough or reach far enough inside myself to find enough holiness to forgive everything that my mind had branded as *unforgivable.* No. *Bucking up* to forgive all the people and all the hurt I had experienced in my very short life was absolutely impossible for me to do in my own strength.

But it is *not* impossible *for* our God…or *with* our God.

### *Nothing is impossible with God.*

Luke 1:37

God was not asking me to *buck up.* God was asking me, crying out to me, to become a *bucket.* A *bucket* that would freely receive and fully accept God's powerful *gift* of forgiveness. Forgiveness towards all those who had inflicted all their brutal, hateful hurts I had suffered. And forgiveness for myself for all the brutal hatred I felt.

God was asking me to be a *bucket* to His word and way. God was asking me to trust Him. To trust that God's bizarre, absolutely counter-intuitive way of doing things is God's absolute fullest measure of His love for me…His love that would bring God's very best to my life.

God was calling me to obey Him. Forgiveness is not optional. It cost Jesus His life. I had already accepted this *gift* of God. This first and greatest freedom for my life. And now God was calling me to be a *bucket* to receive *this forgiveness* towards all others…for all things. God was offering me the *gift* of His second greatest freedom in my life.

But, as with all gifts offered, I had to *choose* whether or not I would accept it...whether or not I would open it and make this gift my own. God would not force His gift on me. I had a *choice* to make.

I could *choose* to turn my back in defiance. I could *choose* to close my hands to God's gift...and *choose* to form them instead into fists to be shaken at God in anger for all that had happened to me. I could *choose* to harden my heart and hold onto all the hatred, the pain, the brokenness and the bitterness that came as natural consequences of my experiences.

Or I could *choose* to be a *bucket* to be filled with the *gift of forgiveness* that God was offering to me. I could *choose* to open my spiritual hands and my heart to receive this gift – to receive God's power to forgive the unforgivable.

And that night, in that corner, I said, *"Yes."*

*Yes...*to opening my heart. *Yes...*to becoming a *bucket. Yes...*to letting God pour in His powerful gift of *this forgiveness.*

And as I yielded my broken heart to be filled with God's healing power of mercy, I was able to completely forgive Mom, Dad, all of my family, The Driver and The Passenger for all that had been so cruelly taken from me and all the ugly things that had been done to me. At that moment, I knew that through this gift of forgiveness, God was setting me free from the powerful bondage that the destructive evil – inflicted on me by others – had held over my life. And God was setting me free from the powerful bondage of the crippling hate that I had for them.

It was almost as if I could hear the heavy chains of pain and fear, hurt and hatred fall clunking down at my feet.

And although I do not comprehend it fully by any means – nor could I at that moment – I believe that not only were spiritual chains broken off from me that night, but that through God's Spirit and His enabling me to extend His unbelievable, counter-intuitive, life-changing forgiveness to others, there were also layers of spiritual chains broken off from my abusers – especially from Mom and Dad. The enemy of God could no longer use me...could no longer hold them bound by any chains of hatred and judgment that came from me. My condemnation of them was gone. Their wrongs were still real. Still ugly and evil. But I would no longer be pointing at them as their accuser. Instead, by God's loving, freeing power, I opened my hands to accept God's gift of forgiveness to cover their sins just as Jesus had done for my sins...for *all* sins on the cross.

In saying, *"Yes,"* to being a *bucket* and to being filled with God's outrageous gift of forgiveness, God was showing me that I was doing things His way...according to His grace and truth...as revealed through the *love* and sacrifice and resurrection of Jesus.

In His pain with the weight of sin tormenting Him, Jesus did not wait for anyone to seek Him out to admit their wrongs or ask for His forgiveness. But right there in the midst of the cruel toll that sin had taken on His life and right then, as sin was actually taking His life, Jesus called out from His nail-embedded, blood-soaked cross,

*"Father, forgive them,*
*for they do not know what they are doing."*
Luke 23:34

And God did. Jesus, God's Holy and Sinless Son, was the full payment for all sin...for all time.

And God was saying to me...*Now you forgive, Sylane...not when it doesn't hurt anymore...not when it is less evil and awful, ugly and sick, hateful and brutal. Sin is, and will always be, evil and awful, ugly and sick, hateful and brutal. Sin will always hurt. Sin will always destroy. But, now you forgive, Sylane, because I have already died for all you have experienced. I have already heard all that you have heard...I have already seen all that you have seen...I have already felt all that you have felt. I have already known it all. I know the destructive power of sin. And I have always hated it all, Sylane. I have hated all the choices of evil that others in your life made against you from the time you were just a little girl, just wanting to twirl around in your beautiful, Princess nightie with its little pink and orange and blue and purple flowers all over it. I have always hated sin. And I have always loved you. You were tiny and helpless and powerless to their choices then. But you are not any longer. And it is exactly because sin is so evil and awful, ugly and sick, hateful and brutal that I chose to die. Through my death, I took on God's full anger and righteous judgment against the evil of sin. And it is through my death...and through my forgiveness...and through my eternal and powerful resurrection, that I have fully conquered all the power of all sin...for all time. And now, Sylane, you forgive. And receive my power, receive my healing, receive my freedom for you...for all time.*

And I said, "*Yes, my God. Yes. I forgive.*" And my spirit, my heart, my mind and my soul were hugged and held and lifted up and twirled around in the mighty and perfect love of my Holy Lord Jesus.

Right then. Right there. On that night. In that corner of Raylene and Jack's apartment.

# 8

## ...they were all filled with the Holy Spirit and spoke the word of God boldly
### Acts 4:31

In those moments of soul wrestling with Raylene's – *with GOD's* – words, *"Now you forgive,"* and then choosing to give my tiny, helpless and powerless self over to being a *bucket* for God's transforming power, my life was turned in...*was twirled in*...the direction towards a truly complete inner healing. A healing so extraordinary and far-reaching that it could only be possible through the Spirit and Word and Love of my Lord Jesus Christ.

Because...*Nothing is impossible with God.*

Including making sure that...my bus route would be changed so that I would become friends with Becky...and be welcomed and loved on by her family...and I would go to Church and Sunday School and Youth Group...and begin growing with others believer-followers of Jesus...and Tim would enter my life at just the right time...and Jack and Raylene would take their new leadership roles with our Youth Group...and Raylene would obediently speak God's transforming words of love and truth: *"Now you forgive"* ...and through my choice to forgive, an unbelievable step would be taken – an unexpected and powerful gift from God would be received – so that I would begin to understand that my *greatest strength* in life would come only from living in the truth that I am completely and utterly, totally and unquestionably *dependent* on the One True God – *dependent* on my Savior and Lord Jesus Christ.

God had lovingly, powerfully shown me the truth of this as He set my spirit, heart, mind and soul firmly on His healing path. God had *twirled me* around in the direction of learning how to live in this God-dependent, ongoing transformation for my fullest strength – for my fullest freedom.

And with me set on this new course – set on this new route, God could now give my school district back their original bus route.

God had changed my heart enough and answered my cry of anguish enough to allow my bus route to be changed back to what it had always been from my first day of kindergarten to my last day of seventh grade. *Bus #52* would, once again, be the bus that would stop at the end of my driveway – beginning again on my first day of ninth grade and continuing on this old, familiar route until my last day as a senior in high school.

For one year, and one year only, God had intervened and interrupted my school district's reasonable and logical bus route so that God's incomprehensible and passionate love could literally save my life from my plan of suicide ...so that God's incomprehensible and passionate love would break through my hurting heart and twisted mind to put me on my God-dependent path towards complete healing and miraculous transformation.

Because...*Nothing is impossible with God.*

What God was doing inside my head and my heart was life-changing and astounding – for me. However, that didn't mean that my life circumstances were changing in the same way, or at the same pace.

Ninth, tenth, eleventh and twelfth grade were still lived out in my home. Still lived out in the midst of the ugliness and sickness of evil and abuse. Still lived out in trying to escape from the cruelty of the touching and the taking, the screaming and the hurting, the utter rejection and deadly disregard. Still lived out in trying to escape from the drunken, drug-induced, evil-spewing threats, the wielding of knives and the terrorization of guns. But escape wasn't always possible.

God's love, His call on my life and the power of God's outrageous, ongoing transformation in me did not allow me to live out my remaining high school years at home by making myself as *distant* as possible or as *invisible* as possible. As I would have liked. As I would have chosen for myself.

No. Our God is a God who comes near. God does not stay distant. Our God is a God who reveals His truth. God does not stay invisible.

And God called me to passionately follow in His *coming-near, truth-revealing* ways. God started in me what I came to refer to as my *Jeremiah-burning-in-my-heart-and-in-my-bones-call-from-God.* I'm pretty sure my family just referred to it as me being obnoxious.

> *If I say, "I will not mention him*
> *or speak any more in his name,"*
> *His word is in my heart like a fire,*
> *a fire shut up in my bones.*
> Jeremiah 20:9

My heart was inflamed and my bones were burning with the truth and the word of God. The Holy Spirit was on me and in me and I *had* to speak the word of God *boldly*.

I could not keep my mouth shut from speaking to Mom and Dad, to My Sister and My Brothers about the love and truth of Jesus Christ. I could not stop the roar within me that urged me to tell them, and tell each of them passionately, all about how much God loves them. All about how much God wants to save them from their sins and heal them from their hurts. I could not shut up about how much I needed…they all needed…we *all* needed the forgiveness that cost Jesus Christ His Holy and Perfect life. I could not shut up about how Jesus could change our lives and heal our family.

To me, this was my *Jeremiah-burning-in-my-heart-and-in-my-bones-call-from-God.* I had to speak to them of Jesus. Out of my love for them. Out of my love for God. Out of my heart-and-bone-burning-crazy-obedience to God.

To my family, this was just me being absolutely obnoxious, annoying, holier-than-thou and judgmental. Out of my mind. Way out of line. And just plain crazy.

And there definitely was some validity to their reactions and perceptions of me. Because there definitely were some radical changes in my behavior – *from* the time immediately after the rape by The Passenger *to* the time God turned…*twirled* me around and placed His crazy *Jeremiah-burning-in-my-heart-and-in-my-bones-call-from-God* on my life.

Immediately after the rape by The Passenger, I had gone pretty quiet at home. I just wanted to avoid the ugly and hurtful in my family as much as I possibly could. I had sunk deep within myself. I had gone off on my bike as much as possible. I had hung out with some of my older, driving, not-such-good-choice-making friends. And I had made lots of not-such-good-choices for myself. Doing things I had no right doing. Drinking and smoking. At one point partying until I could no longer stand...no longer walk. *(Thank you, My Big Sister and My, now-and-since-1975, Brother-In-Law for rescuing me from myself that night.)*

Immediately after the rape by The Passenger, I, the Truth-Teller, became a Liar. Lying about where I was and who I was with. Lying about anything that would keep me away from home. Lying about anything that would shorten any unavoidable conversation with Dad and Mom that could not be otherwise handled with just a monosyllabic response or a quick head nod. But no conversation was ended with Dad or Mom, no escape possible, until I first spoke the requisite phrases of either, *"Yessir"* or *"Yes ma'am"* or *"No-sir"* or *"No ma'am."*

Immediately after the rape by The Passenger, I just didn't even care about making wise or good decisions for my life. I didn't care about my life. I just wanted to stay away from home as much as I possibly could. I just wanted to forget as much as I possibly could.

That was all that mattered in the interim between the rape and the ripping of the suicide note. That was all that mattered in the interim between my planned death and God turning my life around through the power of His love and His forgiveness of me...and the gift of forgiveness that God empowered me to give to my family...to all the people who had hurt me.

And with this turning around of my life – with this *Jeremiah-burning-in-my-heart-and-in-my-bones-call-from-*

*God*, I passionately, desperately wanted my whole family to turn to God…to turn to the Lord Jesus Christ – to turn to His love, His truth, His forgiveness, His hope, His salvation and His transformation for each one of them as individuals and for our family as a whole. I wanted them to turn to Jesus *right now*. And I told them so *boldly*…in every way, at every opportunity that came…or that I forced to come.

This turning around of my life also meant that God reined me in from the partying and the lying, very dramatically and very obviously. God burned in me a strong and focused desire to do things according to God's ways – according to God's good, loving and righteous ways. Those behavior descriptors are not exactly on the-top-ten-list for what most teenagers are looking to do. So, this meant a lot of loneliness. A lot of ridicule. And a lot of rejection for me.

If Jesus was going to be the first love in my life, I would have to deal with the reality that I wasn't going to be first in popularity – I wasn't going to be part of the *in-crowd* or the *cool-crowd* at school. I would have to accept that, from my peers, there wouldn't be a whole lot of love…or phone calls…or invitations to pretty much anything coming my way.

Being a teenager is not always the easiest of life's stages. And being a teenager with a passion and purpose to live for Jesus wasn't making my life a whole lot easier. But God was teaching me to depend fully and only on Him as the true source from where authentic, passionate and unchanging love for me came…as the true source from where unlimited strength, peace and hope came to me.

Jesus knew more about being unwanted, unpopular, ridiculed and rejected than anyone else who ever walked this earth. And Jesus was teaching me, intimately and sternly, to *get over myself.*

Jesus was teaching me through His Holy Spirit and through the Scriptures to be completely and purposefully dependent on Him. Jesus was teaching me to live my life by fully *trusting Him*...not trusting my own strength...not trusting my own feelings...not trusting my visible, tangible circumstances...not even my own perspective.

Jesus, intimately and sternly and always with strong, compassionate love, was teaching me to *trust Him alone.* Even in the midst of the mocking and wounding rejection that came, because of my faith, not only from my peers but from within my family as well.

And the rejection came from My Oldest Brother who was so hurting and angry himself at the time – so involved in drinking, partying and dealing dope at the time – that he could only take so much of his *Jesus Freak* Little Sister talking with him about the love and forgiveness of Jesus Christ without going dangerously ballistic on me. I loved him so much. I wanted the rage and the battle inside of him to stop. I knew that only Jesus could do that. Once My Oldest Brother was out of the house and living in the foster homes during his last two years of high school, his sexual attacks against me, though not his threats, had stopped. And God gave me a boldness – an outrageous, roaring boldness – to tell My Oldest Brother that I loved him and forgave him and that Jesus loved him too. Even more.

More rejection and ridicule, frustration and anger came also from My Big Brother. I gave him plenty of reasons – even though they all came from this overwhelming love God had given me for him. My Big Brother had, at first, gone to Youth Group too. He had that tender heart for God.

But, right then, that's not where he wanted to find his fun and affirmation. He wanted the more tangible and teenage ways to get those. The partying and the girls and the sports and his *bigger-than-life-of-the-party* personality were what gave him what he needed, what he wanted right then.

I loved My Big Brother so much. And I wanted him to grab onto what would really make a difference in his life, what would really fill his heart and his soul – now and for all eternity. Only Jesus could do this for him. Everything else was empty and fleeting. And a lot of it was just plain wrong. And I told him so. Boldly. But My Big Brother was not about to let me get in the way of him having fun – *his way*. He was not about to let me be his judge. And I just needed to *back off* and *shut up* about the love and the way of Jesus. I loved My Big Brother so much. So passionately and persistently much. But to him, right then, I was just *such a pain in the ass.* And I was.

And, for the first time in all our years at home, My Big Sister didn't want anything to do with me. I was different now. Jesus had made such a difference in my life, in my heart, in my mind and in my choices. And to My Big Sister, the difference was just too much and too strong. I felt as though she hated me – or, at least, she seemed to hate this bizarre *talking-about-and-living-for-Jesus* change that had taken place in me. I was not the same Little Sister she had known. Instead, I wanted to make Jesus known to her. Because I loved her so much. Because I loved her so adoringly and so totally much.

My Big Sister had always been my hero, my friend, my fellow *Brownie Elf*. I had always wanted to be like her. But now I wanted to be like Jesus. I couldn't, and didn't want to, follow in her footsteps any longer. I *had* to follow Jesus.

And I wanted My Big Sister to walk with me with Jesus. She had always been there for me. She had always been so good to me. Until, in my unrelenting and uncompromising way, I let My Big Sister know how much I wanted *her* to know and be filled with the goodness and love of Jesus ...and know how much I wanted *her* to be healed from all we had gone through.

But at that time, she wasn't ready to deal with, or even admit to, all we had gone through. At that time, she wasn't ready to deal with the outrageous and unexpected change in me either. It was easier for My Big Sister to just keep her distance – at least emotionally – from me. And it got easier as she graduated from high school...immediately started nursing school...then married my (rescuer) Brother-In-Law just one year after her high school graduation. Our bond, that had been such a safe and sweet place for me, was breaking. And so was my heart. I was so hurt and so angry that God had taken My Big Sister away from me when He took me to Himself in such an all-encompassing way.

But I could do it no other way. This was a season of continual and passionate words and actions and interactions with my family as I was held, intimately and sternly, by the *Jeremiah-burning-in-my-heart-and-in-my-bones-call-from-God* that had been placed on my life.

This is *not* a call that God places on every person who has suffered from abuse. I want that to be deeply and clearly understood. God does not call every person who has suffered abuse to deal with their abusers in this same way as He called me. I was called to stay in their lives intimately and to stay in their faces frequently about Jesus. That was the call that *God* determined to place on me. God knows exactly what His very best plan – His perfect purpose and loving call – is for every one of His children. And that may, and usually does, look very different from one person to another. However, the universal call from our Almighty God to every single one of us, no matter what we may have suffered or to what extent we may have been hurt, is the same: Forgive. Forgive everyone. Forgive everything.

And God's call for me also meant that I *had* to speak to my family about Jesus. There were so many lies, so many hurts, so much ugliness, so much sickness and so much sin in my family. I burned with an urgency and a passion for every member in my family to have a new life in Jesus. I burned with an urgency and a passion that seemed to match the engulfing evil that had been crippling and destroying each and every one of us for so many years.

I knew the truth of Jesus. And I knew His offer of life, full life – for right now and for all eternity. And I also knew the true, single-minded, twisted purpose of the evil – of the enemy-thief – that was desecrating my family. Jesus had made both of these truths so clear when He said:

> *"The thief comes only to steal and kill and destroy;*
> *I have come that they may have life,*
> *and have it to the full."*

John 10:10

And I was filled with the *Jeremiah-burning-in-my-heart-and-in-my-bones-call-from-God* for every member of my family. I wanted them to know Jesus. Now. I did not want to have any portion of our lives stolen or killed or destroyed anymore. I wanted healing for us all. Now. I wanted all of us to live in Jesus. Now.

I just didn't have, at that time, the grace or maturity or patience to shine a *gentle* light towards Jesus and all that

He could do to heal all of our hearts. Because there was *nothing gentle* about the emotional, mental, physical, sexual and spiritual deathblows that had pummeled my family.

And God's call on my life, during those first couple of years after God turned my life around, was far more similar in style to Jeremiah – the confrontative prophet with his *burning-in-my-heart-and-in-my-bones-call-from-God* than it was similar to Joseph of Cyprus who became known as Barnabas – *the Son of Encouragement.*

Only with My Little Brother, at that time, did I get to be more of a Barna*bette* than a Jeremiah. His heart was more tender, more wanting the kind of love that was bigger and deeper and truer than anything this world could offer. And certainly more real and safe than what was offered at home. His partying hard days had not yet begun, and although I was not the star of popularity or coolness, My Little Brother recognized my sincere and passionate love for him. As a ninth grader he joined me (then a junior in high school) in Youth Group and in Church. Making these his own. Tim and I welcomed him as our brother and friend, spending a lot of good times just hanging out and talking together. And My Little Brother opened his heart to a love far more sincere and passionate for him than mine could ever be. My Little Brother opened his heart to the perfect and eternal love of the Lord Jesus Christ.

My Little Brother and I sang together in our Church's Folk Group and (in connection with our Youth Group) we often performed short, poignant dramas for the church congregation. We traveled together to participate in *Lay Witness Missions* – these were outreach events held by churches in our local area where we, along with other youth and adults, told the people that came about the saving truth of Jesus and difference His love had made in our lives. Then, just before my high school years ended, My Little Brother and I had the extra sweet bonding experience of being in, and testifying to the truth and joy of Jesus Christ through, my senior play *Godspell*.

With Mom and Dad, while I was still in high school – and after God twirled me around and filled me with an overwhelming love and forgiveness for them and that over-powering, crazy *Jeremiah-burning-in-my-heart-and-in-my-bones-call-from-God* – they, too, like My Sister and My Brothers, were in the path of truth that God was burning in me...to tell to them.

It was now Mom and Dad's turn to want to escape. But God wouldn't let them...and God wouldn't let me let them escape. Even when it wasn't easy for me. Even when it was scary. Even when it raised the danger and anger levels to ugly places. Even when I wanted to throw up and just quit trying. God wouldn't let me. Because God loved me. And because God loved Mom and Dad and all of my family with a love that we cannot even begin to fathom.

And God is a persistent, persevering God.

And God called me to persist and persevere in prayer for each and every one of my family members. To persist and persevere in talking with them about Jesus...writing to them about Jesus...living out my life around them in this all-encompassing, purpose-driven relationship with Jesus.

My Oldest Brother was right. I was a *Jesus Freak*. However, I prefer the term *fool for Christ* a bit more. It was God's love and power and the *Jeremiah-burning-in-my-heart-and-in-my-bones-call-from-God* that kept me in this persistent, persevering, *foolish* place.

*We have been made a spectacle to the whole universe,*
*to angels as well as to men. We are fools for Christ.*
1 Corinthians 4:9-10

*For the message of the cross [of Jesus]*
*is foolishness to those who are perishing,*
*but to us who are being saved it is the power of God.*
1 Corinthians 1:18

And so, in the persistent and persevering power of God, I made an absolutely foolish spectacle of myself as a fool for Christ *with* my family…and *for* my family.

Not too long after ripping up my suicide note and God's twirling me around, I *foolishly* wrote out a letter to Mom and Dad.

I wrote to Mom and Dad to tell them how much I loved them. That God loved them. I told them I had forgiven them completely. And I told them *completely* for what I had forgiven them. I called the incest *incest.* I called the abuse *abuse.* These *words* had never been used or spoken aloud about what had been happening in my family. These *sins* in my family had never been admitted to. Incest and Abuse had never been called – or called out for – what they really were.

In this letter, I told Mom and Dad that I could no longer, would no longer, live a lie. I could no longer, would no longer, pretend to anyone that we were a big, happy family. Our family was horribly sick and needed healing. Our family was engrossed in evil and needed forgiveness. This was their fault. This was their choice. And it was time to make a different choice. Accept the love God has for them. Confess their sins. Accept the full forgiveness of Jesus. Accept the full salvation and the new life that Jesus alone can offer them. It was not yet too late.

I wrote and *begged* Mom and Dad to let Jesus forgive them and save them. I wanted them to know God's love and God's power and God's amazing renewal. I begged them to do this because, as I wrote in the letter, *"Mom and Dad, I don't ever want to be eternally separated from you. I want us to spend eternity together with Jesus. I love you and I always will."*

I foolishly wrote this letter. Then, I even more foolishly gave them this letter. I had prayed – persistently and with perseverance – before writing it, while writing it, in the giving of it to them and in the waiting for their responses.

Mom's response, from what I could figure from her silence, was mostly a stunned shock. At first, the surprise of my directness about the incest and abuse and about Jesus being her only hope and salvation seemed to cause Mom's big, round blue eyes to get even bigger and rounder. Then, Mom's eyes narrowed to her well-known, and way too familiar, *hate-glare* towards me. A look, a stare, that had come at me and attacked me many times before and would come at me and attack me many times in the days and years to follow. But, right then, there were no *outward* words that came from Mom to me about my letter of love and forgiveness to her and Dad.

Dad's response needed no figuring out. He made himself perfectly clear. Towering over me. Raising his hand to me. His face clenched and seething with rage.

*"You goddamn little bitch! Don' you never come up aginst me like that agin, in your holier-than-thou-goddamn-attitude! You an' that goddamn letter of yours can both go to hell! If I ever wants your goddamn opinion 'bout anything, I will goddamn be sure to ask fo' it! An' I goddamn for sure don' never wants to hear not one more*

*goddamn peep from you 'bout any of your religious crap!*
*Not ever! D'ya hear me?"*

I stood there outwardly calm as he screamed and condemned me. I just looked at Dad. Listened to Dad. He hated me even more. He had missed the love of God...he had missed my foolishly, passionately motivated love for him and for Mom that had caused me to write that letter.

Dad's raised hand, however, did not miss my face as it smashed into my left cheek with all the force of his hate. Dad stormed out. I ran into my room, locked the door and sank. I sank and I sobbed. I sank into a place of pity and hurt and helplessness.

It took a few days for God to pull me out of that sink hole so that I could go about and enter back into the *normal* in my life again...enter back into the *normal* in my life outside of my home...with classes and homework, after school activities, Youth Group and hanging out with the few close friends I had. And for awhile, I just stayed quiet again whenever I was at home with Mom and Dad, with My Sister and My Brothers. I didn't talk about Jesus. I just didn't talk at all. About anything. Or, at least, as little as I could possibly get away without talking over the next several weeks.

I had to recover. I had expected a different response from Mom and Dad. From My Sister and My Brothers. I had expected that they would *get it*. *Get* the love and forgiveness and salvation and healing that comes from Jesus alone. They didn't *get it*. And I didn't *get why* they didn't *get it*.

And it hurt. So much. So soul-wrenching, heart-breaking much.

One way that God put some *normal* in my very abnormal teenage life was through a new weekly routine I committed to during the last half of my ninth grade year. I had gone to the Pastor of our Church to ask if I could be baptized. I knew enough Scripture now to know that, although baptism was not necessary for my salvation, believers were baptized to publicly profess and confirm their faith in Jesus. And I felt compelled to do the same – to declare that I had placed my faith and my life in the hope and promise given through the death and resurrection of Jesus.

My Pastor said, *"Yes, you can be baptized. But, first, you need to go through some coursework that youth usually go through together as a group in eighth grade."* And so for a couple of hours once a week after school for the next several weeks, my Pastor and I went through filmstrips and study books and Scripture to prepare me, according to the requirements of the First United Methodist Church, for the Sacrament of Baptism.

God had kept me moving forward in my growth in Jesus in some pretty bizarre ways. It certainly did make me a *fool for Christ.* My public baptism was one of those ways to not only declare my faith in Jesus to my new church family (many of whom had lovingly welcomed me, as *foolish* as I may have seemed), but my baptism also gave me the opportunity to speak about Jesus, once again, in my home more openly. I invited my family to come to church with me on the day I was to be baptized.

Mom came.

On June 2, 1974, Mom came to church with me. She sat with me and she watched as I walked myself up the church aisle (as I would do so again six years later in this same

Church when I married my Timmy) to stand alone before the Pastor, before *God*, before all the people in our church and choose to declare my faith in Jesus as my Savior and Lord and be baptized *"in the name of the Father, and of the Son, and of the Holy Spirit. Amen."*

I was so thankful. So happy Mom had come with me. Been there for me. This was huge. We didn't talk about it much. So much awkwardness stood between us. So much was left unsaid. But I told Mom how much it meant to me that she had come to see me baptized.

I told Mom, *"I love you. I love you so much. Thank you so much for being here with me."*

*"I love you, too, Sylane."* And we hugged. And we didn't say much more. Mom just drove us back home, back over *The Little Bridge* that crosses the river that runs behind our house…and life at home was just *a little bit* different.

Though never spoken, never really expressed, I think Mom saw in me, on that day, a strength, a tenacity of spirit and an intelligence – that were actually pretty similar to her own. *(Oh! Antinomy!)* And again, though never spoken or expressed, I believe that God used, on that day, my sincerity of faith and love for God and for Mom and for my whole family to make life at home just *a little bit* different.

That *little bit* of difference was *significant* in the sexual realm.

From the time the Social Worker took a report on My Oldest Brother, to process him into the Foster Home system, the brutal rapes I had experienced from him stopped. God pushed me to make sure that, although he was out of the home, my love for him and showing him that love never stopped. And neither did my *Jeremiah-burning-*

*in-my-heart-and-in-my-bones-call-from-God.* To love on My Oldest Brother, in my *Jesus Freak* kind of way, I called him. I wrote to him. I met with him, but only in public places or at Grandma and Grandpa's house or at our house on holidays or up at Racquette Lake. Because of God's love, I wanted to stay in My Oldest Brother's life. I wanted to keep telling him of Jesus, His love, forgiveness and salvation. But I didn't *ever* want to give My Oldest Brother the chance to rape me again. I had to always stay alert. And yet, I also always had to stay loving and reaching out to him. That was God's *foolish*, precarious call on my life. A balance that only the grace and truth of Jesus could help me find.

Not long after my baptism, Dad's coming to take from me sexually, coming to touch me and rape me also stopped. But Dad's crude, suggestive talk never stopped. And I never stopped being on my guard around Dad either. Not while living at home. I always walked a wide berth around him. I always backed up an extra few feet when we spoke. I tried never to be in the house alone with Dad. Not even in the same room alone with him. If I could help it.

I'm not sure why Dad's sexual assaults against me stopped. Was it his fear that I would tell the authorities, now that the Social Worker had been told by Mom and Dad, but not by me, of My Oldest Brother's sexual assaults against me? Was it fear that I could get pregnant? Dad stopped his assaults against me before I had my ovarian surgery at age fifteen, before the doctor's pronouncement that I probably could not have any children of my own. Was it because Dad had seen, though never admitted to, the devastation of me as a twelve year old after the rape by The Passenger? Was it because I had named *incest* and *abuse* for what they were – both face-to-face and in my letter – and, yet, still offered Dad forgiveness and love through the power of Jesus?

I don't know. I don't know why Dad's sexual violence against me and the touching and taking, grabbing and groping of me by his hands covered with those long, black hairs and his cut-off trigger finger had finally stopped. I was just so glad it did.

I needed this *significant* difference to take place in my life...to take place in my home. I needed some protection of my body and my being. And I needed God to start healing my head from the horribly twisted view of sexuality and men that I had.

I was so thankful for this *significant* difference.

But I wanted it *all* to be different right away. I wanted every heart to change right away. I wanted, in my home and in each member of my family, for the prophecy from Scripture to come true right away...

> *...That at the name of Jesus every knee should bow,*
> *in heaven and on earth and under the earth,*
> *and every tongue confess that Jesus Christ is Lord,*
> *to the glory of God the Father.*
> Philippians 2:10-11

But it didn't happen right away.

# 9

## *"Do you want to get well?"*
### *John 5:6*

I had desperately wanted, passionately hoped, boldly and *foolishly* acted in every way I possibly could to help bring about the complete healing and change in my family…right away.

So, when the subsequent insane, dangerous and evil bouts of Dad's booze-drenched, narcotic-driven, fist-beating, gun-shooting, life-threatening explosions came, I was not well-prepared. Even though this is what I had always known, I was no longer prepared for this kind of evil to go unchecked. My life with Jesus had made such a difference to me. And I had expected something different. Right away.

I had expected Dad and Mom and all of my family to *get it*. I had opened my heart, opened my faith, opened my mouth to share about Jesus – His love, His forgiveness, His salvation. I had persistently, perseveringly been praying for my family every day. And I wasn't about to stop. But Dad didn't *get it*. Mom didn't *get it*. Except for My Little Brother, during his early high school years, no one else in my family seemed to *get it*. And I didn't *get why* they didn't *get it*.

It hurt. So much. So soul-wrenching, heart-breaking much. And when these bouts came, I sank. I sank and I sobbed. I sank into a deep place of pity and hurt and helplessness.

And God would, once again, have to pull me out of my sink hole – to trust His love for me, to walk with Him in courage and in my *Jeremiah-burning-in-my-heart-and-in-my-bones-call-from-God* so that I could keep telling about and living out the love of Jesus with my family...until my heart would break again...until I would, once again, sink and sob, entering into my place of pity and hurt and helplessness...and God would, once again, have to pull me out of my sink hole...

After Timmy and I had become best friends and then began dating, I told him a little bit at a time about my family situation. About the violence, the anger, the drugs and the alcohol. About my sadness and my hurt.

I didn't tell Tim about the incest for a few years yet. That was still too hard to talk about. Too sick, too embarrassing, too awful. God still had so much healing to work in my life from the sickness and the evil of my family's incest and being raped by The Passenger. All those feelings were compounded and confused as I was now experiencing my own natural sexual attraction towards someone I truly loved and with whom I needed to work through, and build, the righteous boundaries of sexuality. *(We didn't always choose to build and keep those righteous boundaries very well. I thank God for His forgiving grace and His truth that intimately and sternly always called us back to do things His way – to keep Jesus always at the very center of our relationship. And through God's good love and outrageous, unlimited power to heal, Tim and I have long been able to experience and enjoy the beautiful, powerful, freeing, passionate and intimate gift of sexuality that God had always intended for a husband and a wife to share. Thank You, Lord, for Your amazing gift! Thank You, Lord, for Your amazing and full healing that You gave to me to enjoy Your gift!)*

But during our first bit of time together, I *did* tell Tim about how much I wanted my family to *get it – get* the love of Jesus. *Get* God's love, forgiveness and salvation. And with Tim, I poured out my heartbreak and let him see me in my sinking and my sobbing sink hole that I entered into because I didn't *get why* my family didn't *get it.*

Timmy *alone* saw how very hard God's call of love was on me. Tim saw the depth of sadness that I would sink into after a difficult and frustrating time with Mom and Dad or with one of My Siblings…when they just weren't *getting it*…when they just weren't *getting Jesus.*

And Tim, with his faith in God and his love for me, wrote a song to let me know that he heard my broken heart for my family. One summer day while we were at the beach, Tim played that song on his guitar while he sang it to me in his beautiful, deep bass, *my-favorite-sound-in-the-world* voice.

Part of Tim's song, "There's An Answer," was his way to encourage me to keep trusting God no matter how much heartbreak I felt or how ugly my circumstances seemed…to keep trusting in Jesus even when I just couldn't even begin to *get why* people and life were the way they were.

*If it seems that your family is falling apart…*
*And what you see is breaking your heart*
*Look to the One who will make your family whole…*
*Look to the One who saved your soul*

*There's an Answer....Just Remember, there's an Answer*
*There's an Answer...To your prayer*

*If it seems there is no love around...*
*And that beauty cannot be found*
*Look to the One who gave you so much love...*
*To find Him, you just look above*
*There's an Answer....Just Remember, there's an Answer*
*There's an Answer...To your prayer*

*The One I speak of is Jesus our Lord...*
*The One who gave us His Word*
*That when we have a question, just look to the sky...*
*And ask Jesus, why?*
*There's an Answer....Just Remember, there's an Answer*
*There's an Answer...To your prayer*

Tim's love and his song had reminded me that my call from God was to keep on praying for each and every person in my family. There would be an answer to my prayer. For now and for always that answer is to trust my Lord Jesus. No matter what.

And my call from God was also to keep loving on each and every person in my family *and* to keep on sharing the love of Jesus with them in whatever ways I could. No matter what.

To pray for and love on my family was not just a call from God when I lived at home. I was not ever released from this call from God. Not when I went to college. Not when Tim and I were married and lived in Rochester, New York. Not when we had two beautiful daughters. Not when we moved to France. Not when we moved to California ...or back to New York...or to Pennsylvania...or to New Jersey. I was never released from God's call to do things God's way. None of us are.

And God's way is always the way of Love. True. Caring. Sacrificial. *No matter what…*Love.

*Love your enemies*
*and pray for those who persecute you...*
Matthew 5:43

But that doesn't mean it's easy to love…or that love is ever returned.

During my years after graduating from high school and going onto college (for my first year at Keuka College in the Finger Lakes area of New York, then graduating with my Bachelors Degree in Sociology, Psychology and Spanish after two more years at Potsdam State University in New York), God's call on my life: To give and tell of the love of Jesus and share the truth of His salvation with my family…and others – was absolutely the same. And it wasn't always easy…at all.

I took out loans to pay for my college education. I didn't want the bizarre and controlling behavior that came, especially from Dad – and often about money, to have any twisted claims or rights to manipulate me anymore than I had already been. Dad, in his warped thinking, could blame me for *taking and stealing* his money if I had asked for his financial help. Student loans meant going into debt for a time and paying some interest fees. But they also meant some much needed independence and freedom for me. And a good deal of peace of mind.

And I believe that *not* asking Dad and Mom for any college money actually gave them some relief and made my relationship with them a little less complicated. Attitudes and perceptions about money can really poison and complicate all kinds of relationships. And it did, horribly so, in my family.

But going off to college, even on my own dime, didn't free me from the call God had for me with my family. God's Spirit made it very clear that I was to stay in an active, intentional relationship and frequent communication with everyone in my family. Especially with Mom and Dad. God's call continued to be that I love them and pray for them, share the love of Jesus with them, write letters often, go home over vacation and semester breaks and make phone calls home weekly.

Doing things this way was actually God's gift of love *to me*. Obedience to God's good and loving ways is always a gift to us. It's just not always easy.

Every time before I wrote a letter, called on the phone or made a visit home, I would have to take some serious and focused time in prayer, often fasting as well, to ask God to help me love, to help me be wise, to help me be strong, to help me…just *help me, God.* I could not love, really love Mom and Dad, My Sister and My Brothers without the love of Jesus…without the help of Jesus.

One phone call home in May of 1980 with Mom was especially heartbreaking and maddening for me – no matter how well I had prepared and *pre-prayered* myself for this conversation.

Just about one and a half weeks before my graduation from Potsdam State University and two and a half weeks before Tim and I were to be married, I found out that Dad had gone into one of his most violent, dramatic and very public episodes of drunken rage. I was finishing my college finals, but had stopped studying for a bit to call Mom. I had felt something was especially *not right*. So when I called, I told Mom that my spirit was very unsettled for our family.

Mom spoke in very even tones, saying, *"I didn't want to worry you before your graduation, but yes, something has happened."*

Mom went on to explain, *"Dad is back at Marcy* (a regional mental hospital) *for a few days. He had gotten very violent and tried to kill me. I had to run to the neighbors' house in the middle of the night. Dad was so bad this time that I knew I had to have the police help me get him somewhere so he could get settled down. But it got worse because Dad boarded up the doors and barricaded himself in the house. He had a shoot-out with the police before he finally surrendered to them."* Mom was still speaking in eerily even tones. *"It will all be okay, though. Dad will be fine and back home in just a few days. He'll be back before your graduation and before your wedding. It will all be okay."*

Only by the holy power of God was I able to answer with a calm voice, even as everything in my head was screaming out against the ugly evil and the ugly lies of my family. God held my head, my heart and my tongue in those moments, in a bit of a spiritual-emotional vise-grip. And I was able to respond gently but strongly, *"Mom, you need to sign Dad into Marcy so that he will be forced to stay there and get some real help finally. Mom, you can't just have Dad come back home. It's not fine. It's not okay. Mom, it's not good for you. It's not good for Dad. Please, Mom, sign him in so that he has to stay. Mom, this could be the chance for some real healing to happen for Dad and for all of us. Mom, please don't let the doctors let him out. I know you have the authority and influence that could get the doctors to see how much Dad needs some real, long-*

*term therapy. Mom, this could be God's way of opening the door for His healing to come in."*

Mom was not happy with me.

Her voice was no longer even, it had turned hard and cold now. *"Sylane, don't you think I know what I'm doing? I know I'm a stupid, no-good-son-of-a bitch!* (This was one of Mom's most repeated refrains whenever I tried to talk with her about any of our family's problems.) *But! I am not asking for your holier-than-thou opinion. You asked me what was happening. I told you. And that's that. Dad will be home and everything will be just fine in a few days. He just got a little too drunk."*

*"Mom, I love you. I just want what's best for you and for Dad."*

*"Sylane, that's enough. I'm done talking with you."*

The conversation was done. I told Mom I loved her. I would be praying for her. She hung up first. I hung up. *Then*, I let the rage come…and it came more fully and destructively than I had ever expected or imagined. I overturned my dorm room dresser, my desk and my bed in my frenzied rage. I threw books and blankets and clothes and smashed my lamp onto the floor. It was a very good thing that I was living in *a single* without a roommate during my senior year. The bill for the damaged property could have been higher than the student loans I had taken out. Say nothing about how damaging my destructive outburst could have been to a roommate relationship.

I ran out of my room, slamming my door with such force that it bounced back open. And I ran. I ran for the next three hours. I ran and I cried and I screamed and I prayed for God to *help me*…to *heal my family*…and I ran until I couldn't run anymore. Then, I just walked back to my room, and with some worried friends as spectators, I spent the next several hours calmly cleaning up the destruction zone that had once been my room.

Dad did get out of Marcy in a few days. Mom and Dad both came to my college graduation, although Mom hadn't told me Dad was coming. He came to *surprise* me. And he did.

I should have just been so thankful that they had made this very big effort to come. My Big Brother and My Little Brother had come too. I wanted to shake off the insanity of how my family denied problems and ignored our painful reality. I wanted to show *only* how thankful I was that these four had made this sacrifice of time and travel (three hours by car from our hometown) to come to my graduation ceremony.

But I was stunned.

I not only had to get my graduation cap to stay on my head that day, I had to ask God to keep holding my head with His eternal perspective, and hold it exceedingly tightly in His love so that I could focus *only* on the good truth that they had come. That Mom, Dad, My Big Brother and My Little Brother had come to be with me on this special day. *Help me, God,* to hold onto that good truth…while not buying into the lies that hold our family so tightly.

A few days after graduation, I packed up, left Potsdam and headed back home. With just one more week before my wedding to Tim, I asked Dad if I could talk with him. I felt so sick inside because I didn't know what I might be facing. But after much time of *pre-prayering*, I knew that I could not live a lie on my wedding day. God had given me so much peace about the decision I had come to. And in that peace of God, I spoke softly and calmly to Dad.

I told Dad that I loved him very much. I told Dad that I did not make this choice easily...nor did I make it to hurt him...I made it to be true to myself...I told Dad that I could not have him *give me away* at my wedding...I didn't feel like I was ever his...and I needed to *walk myself* down the aisle. I asked Dad to understand my decision. I told him that I very much wanted him to be with us at our wedding ...that his being part of this day was very important to me. And yet, for me, I needed to live...and walk down the aisle *by myself*...in the truth. I was not angry with him...I wasn't trying to hurt or punish him in any way. I wanted him to understand that.

God had obviously gone way ahead of me on this one because Dad actually looked at me the whole time I was speaking. Neither his anger nor his voice rose. Dad just simply said, with an unusual softness and calm in his words, *"Laney, if that's what you want then that's aw-right by me."*

*Oh, my goodness. Thank You, God. You are amazing.*

Mom, on-the-other-hand was, at first, very angry with *holier-than-thou-little* me. *What would people think?* But, eventually, Mom also accepted my decision. I'm pretty sure the fact that the guests *only* included about thirty close family members from both Tim's family and mine probably helped spare Mom from too much embarrassment. She could just blame this bizarre break with tradition on my pigheaded, stubborn, independent streak. I was okay with that.

It was probably about three in the morning on the day of my wedding, when I was wakened suddenly by My Big Brother laughing and putting his head and most of his big, burly body inside my room. He had just come in from some partying, and needed to ask me something, *"Hey, do you know what that Big Cookie was in the kitchen? It wasn't very sweet. But I ate most of it anyway."*

I sat up a little shocked, but not really. This was, after all, My Big Brother. I explained to him, laughing a little bit too, and mostly shaking my head, *"That Big Cookie you just ate was the unleavened bread I had made for Tim's and my wedding Communion."*

My Big Brother sat down with a thump on the side of my bed, and looking into my face, he put one hand up to his mouth and with a big silly grin, just said, "Uh-oh!"

And for the next hour or so, My Big Brother and I had one of our beautiful, deep and honest talks that I treasure so much. We talked about our family – still in pretty big generalities; specifics were just too hard to really talk about. We talked about the judgments and misjudgments we had of each other. And we forgave each other. We talked about God and His love. And we told each other that we *really* did love each other. And we both cried…just a little…and we hugged.

My Big Brother went to his room. I heard him fall hard onto his bed. I tucked myself back in, *thanking God* for the beautiful thing He had done by helping us take those wee steps towards breaking down some of the lies and some of the walls of pain and judgment between My Big Brother and me.

And God had done this beautiful thing in the wee hours of that morning. The morning of my wedding day.

A few hours later, I got up extra early to bake another loaf of unleavened bread for our wedding Communion. And I smiled and thanked God the whole time…and shook my head just a little...because My Big Brother had eaten *that Big Cookie.*

As the wedding began, My Big Sister and I hugged each other in the back of church, really hugged each other in a way that I had missed so much for a very long time. And as my Matron of Honor, My Big Sister walked ahead of me down the aisle. And on that day, on my wedding day, I was so thankful to be, once again, following in the footsteps of My Big Sister.

Then it was my turn, and although it *looked* like I walked myself down that wedding aisle, I was walking with my Jesus. And He wasn't going to give me away. His plan was to join together, even more deeply and intimately, with Tim and me in our marriage.

As Jesus and I walked down the aisle to meet Tim at ten o'clock in the morning on June 7, 1980, My Little Brother lovingly sang, "Morning Has Broken," with just a trace of some emotional cracks in his voice.

And for Tim and me, it truly was like a first morning...like a new day. And I believe that for my family, in some ever so subtle emotional-spiritual ways, it was like a first morning...like a new day for them too...as they saw and heard Tim and me sing "Longer Than" to each other (A decision we had made just the night before!)...as we took our marriage vows – making promises to each other and to God about our life-long, love-commitment to each other...as we shared Communion with that second *Big Cookie*...and as we walked back down the aisle together as husband and wife...with Jesus.

It was a small wedding in terms of the number of guests. But the wedding itself was big on exuding the big love and big peace and big hope of our God…who makes everything new.

And just to keep me balanced and humbled, I suppose, on the drive over to our wedding brunch, My Little Brother just happened to *moon* us – with just a tad too much encouragement from My Big Brother. But, hey! That's part of the antinomy and the humor of their own personal life stories.

Now married, and thankfully so, to my Tim, God's call for me to stay in relationship – to keep loving on each and every person in my family and to keep praying for them *continually* and to keep sharing the love of Jesus with them in whatever ways I could – did not diminish.

So, that meant phone calls and letters and visits to their homes and invitations for them to come to ours. My call from God was the same: Love them. Really love them because of the love of Jesus. No matter what.

And sometimes, even if I had *pre-prayered*, the hurt from the responses I got – whether cool, cold or cruel – would just be so hard on my heart.

It was during those times that the pull from the pain of my family not *getting it*…not *getting* the love of Jesus would, once again, take me down. And the crying would start…and the crying would turn to sobbing…until I would, once again, sink and sob, entering into my place of pity and hurt and helplessness.

Often after an especially painful encounter, Timmy would hold up pillows for me to pummel and beat on with all my might so I could let out my hurt and frustration. And as I landed one ferocious blow after another on those innocent pillows, I would be crying, yelling and absolutely swallowed up by the hurt in my heart.

*"Why don't they get it? When are they ever going to change? When are they going to get it? I'm doing everything I can possibly do! I'm loving them. I'm praying for them. I'm writing to them. I'm calling them. I'm visiting them. I haven't turned my back on them...even when I've wanted to. God won't let me. I keep on loving them. I keep sharing the love of Jesus with them! When are they ever going to get it?!"*

Timmy would stand there calmly, and in his deep spiritual and physical strength, he would hold those pillows securely as I beat the stuffing out of them. With Tim *alone* I could scream out and punch out the depth of my frustration and hurt. And Tim would lovingly, faithfully absorb the blows from all the pain that I was jamming into those pillows...all the pain that was coming out of my broken heart. Tim was my safe place where I could let all of the stink from my sink hole be released.

That is until one day.

We were well into the first year of our marriage, and I had just gotten off the phone with Mom. (If Dad ever answered the phone when I called, he would, upon hearing my voice, say, *"Here's your Mother."* Nothing else. Just, *"Here's your Mother."* And immediately Dad would pass the phone to Mom.) That particular day's call with Mom had been especially painful as some very cold and cutting words came from her and were breaking my heart. Only by God's strong love holding me (and my mouth) very tightly, was I able to close our conversation with any semblance of grace and maturity. *"I love you, Mom. I'm praying for you and Dad. God bless you both."*

That day, as soon as I hung up, I just let the full flood of pain hit me and all my sobbing questions rise. *"Why don't they get it? When are they ever going to change? When are they going to get it?"* Timmy had taken his faithful stance with the war-worn pillows, but after just a few seconds of letting my punches hit their mark, Tim pulled the pillows away and took a step back. He looked at me with his big, brown-green eyes and in *my-favorite-sound-in-the-world* voice of his, Tim asked me something that I did not want to hear.

*"Do you want to be happy?"*

I was dumbfounded and in shock. Just as I had been, initially, on that night in the corner when Raylene had confronted me with the words, *"Now you forgive."*

I had no words that came immediately. I just stared at Tim. My mouth finally formed into a questioning circle, asking him, *"What?!"*

Tim asked again, *"Sylane, do you want to be happy?"*

Unlike the night in the corner with Raylene, that day I had an escape route. So I took it. I ran straight into the bathroom, slammed the door, locking it shut. I threw any God-acquired grace and maturity (I might have had) right out the window. I started screaming and stomping my feet and shaking my fists in the air and fuming out in a crazed fit of hurt, anger and indignation.

*"How dare he ask me, 'Do you want to be happy?' Who does he think he is? 'Do you want to be happy?' I am the happiest damn person I know! Especially considering all that I've been through! How dare he not allow me some time just to get my feelings out! I have every right to hurt when things are hurtful! I have every right to be sad because my family still doesn't get it...still doesn't get how much Jesus loves them! He has no right to be asking me of all people, 'Do you want to be happy?'"*

Tim's words had cut deeply into my heart.

In the midst of all my fuming and fussing, a hush and the powerful authority of the Spirit of God came over me, right there in that bathroom. My heart was pierced. Words similar to Timmy's words were rising up and dissecting me. God's Spirit flooded me with His presence and cut me deeply with the quiet, stern, challenging – yet loving beyond description – words of Jesus himself.

Words that Jesus had spoken to a man who had been crippled for thirty-eight years. To that invalid man, Jesus did *not* ask his usual questions of: *"Do you believe I can make you well? Do you have faith that I can heal you?"* Instead, Jesus asked that man, as He was pointedly and poignantly asking me right then in that bathroom,

### *"Do you want to get well?"*

John 5:9

The cutting and piercing of my heart by these words spoken by Jesus forced me to confront myself very honestly. Very humbly. Timmy's words spoken gently, yet with the courage that only true love has, held up a mirror to the truth that I was still holding onto my own crippling thoughts. I was not a physical invalid. But I was still allowing the mentality of being a victim – an unloved, hurt and rejected victim – to have way too much power over me.

I had to come to terms with the *full* truth – that I had only *partially* revealed through my tirades of: *"Why don't they get it? When are they ever going to change? When are they going to get it? When are they ever going to get the love Jesus has for them?"*

My heart was truly broken for each and every person in my family that had not yet come to accept the love and salvation of Jesus. Jesus didn't have a problem with *this part* of my heartbreak. His heart was broken for them because of this too.

Jesus had to show me *the rest* of the *full* truth that I had not spoken aloud and had held onto so tightly…for so long. *The rest* of the *full* truth was: My hurt and my sobbing and my choice to enter…and re-enter into my sink hole – into my place of pity and hurt and helplessness over the years – was *not* caused *just* from Mom and Dad and My Siblings *not getting* Jesus and *not getting* His love.

No. I had to admit that *the rest* of the *full* truth for the cause of my pain was coming from me. Because *I was allowing* deep self-pity to keep me entrapped. Because *I was focusing* my attention on all the hurt I felt because …*Mom and Dad and My Siblings didn't get me. Didn't love me. Not the way they should love me. Not the way I deserved to be loved. Mom and Dad didn't get me. And my little heart wanted to be gotten.*

This was, ultimately, *the rest* of the *full* truth that was breaking my heart. *I was keeping* me an emotional cripple. No one else. *I was keeping* me thinking and acting like a victim. No one else. *My choice* of remaining – feeling like…thinking like…acting like – a victim because of my family's lack of love towards me, was what was breaking my heart. Not them. It was *me*. It was my choice.

And Tim saw this.

And Jesus would have no more of this. I had to answer Him. *"Do you <u>want</u> to get well?"* God's Spirit kept bringing God's truths, God's words to my mind. And God kept cutting through the lies of victimhood that *I had allowed* to keep me hostage…that *I had allowed* to keep breaking my heart.

*For the word of God is living and active.*
*Sharper than any double-edged sword,*
*it penetrates even to dividing soul and spirit,*
*joints and marrow; it judges the thoughts*
*and attitudes of the heart.*

Hebrews 4:12

Tim had asked, *"Sylane, do you want to be happy?"* Jesus was asking, *"Sylane, do you want to get well?"* And the Spirit of God was making it perfectly clear to me that just as accepting the *gift of God's forgiveness* for my own sins and the sins inflicted on me by others was a *choice,* so too would it be a *choice* for me to accept this *gift of freedom* that God was offering me. Freedom from the heavy, deadly chains of emotional victimhood that were twisting my mind.

I had a choice to make. Again.

I had a choice to make about whether or not I trusted Jesus to break my chains of victimhood.

I had a choice to make about whether or not I believed God's word was true when He said...

*...in all things we are more than conquerors*
*through him who loved us.*

Romans 8:37

God's Spirit was letting me know unequivocally that I could not be a victim and a conqueror at the same time. It is impossible. If I were to choose to be *more than a conqueror* in Jesus then I could no longer remain a victim, an emotional cripple, because of the lack of love I received from my family. Choosing to remain in my victimhood would be a rejection of God's truth and the unfailing, sacrificial love that Jesus Christ poured out to me, and for me, to make me *more than a conqueror* in Him.

Even more, I had a choice to make about whether or not I *wanted* – whether or not I was *willing* to give up every right I had to enter into my pain and enter into my sobbing sink hole. I had a choice to make about whether or not I *wanted* – whether or not I was willing to give up my identity as a victim...and to give up every vestige of victimhood.

Again, I sensed the Spirit of my Jesus asking me, uncompromisingly, to *choose*, "*Do you want to get well?*"

And I knew this was God's powerful way of *doing something* even more about my anguish. This was God's powerful way of *doing something* even more to answer all of my heart-broken prayers. This was my God's powerful way of offering me His uncompromising, healing love to set me even more fully *free*.

A choice had to be made. And the choice was to, once again, and even more fully, become a *bucket* to receive this powerful *gift of freedom*...this gift of God to be *more than a conqueror* through the unconditional, unfailing – and, yes – uncompromising love of my Lord Jesus Christ.

I had a life-transforming, *bucket* choice to make. A God-twirling-me-around choice to make.

And I said, "*Yes, my Lord. Yes. I do want to get well. I do want to be happy. Yes, my Jesus. Yes. I give up all of my rights to be a victim. YOU died for all of my hurts. YOU died for all of my rejections. Yes, my God. Yes. I choose the power and the position of being more than a conqueror through Your love.*"

I chose to be a *bucket* for the healing and the power and the freedom that Jesus had wanted to give to me all along ...that only my Lord Jesus could ever have given to truly transform my life.

I said, *"Yes,"* to my Lord. And my spirit, my heart, my mind and my soul were hugged and held and lifted up, twirled around...*and set even more free*...in the mighty and perfect love of my Holy Lord Jesus.

Right then. Right there. On that day. In that bathroom.

# *10*

## *For I am CONVINCED that…*
## *nothing in all creation will be able to*
## *separate us from the love of God that*
## *is in Christ Jesus our Lord*
### *Romans 8:38*

Loved…I am loved *no matter what*. I am loved by my God.

And years after I had been twirled around in that bathroom to trust, even more, in God's mighty and perfect love for me, God gave me a beautiful, living illustration of this kind of complete, and absolutely necessary, trust in God's love – that I should always have. This time God did it on a train.

When our little Erin was just three years old, she made a very bold and totally spontaneous profession of faith about the love she knew Tim and I – her Mommy and Daddy – had for her.

*No matter what.*

We lived in France at the time, in Chalon-sur-Saone, and the four of us – Tim, three year old Erin, almost one year old Julia and I – were taking the three hour train trip from our home up to Paris. With Erin's red-curly-haired-head resting on my lap and her beautiful, deer-shaped green eyes looking up into mine, Erin began to sing-song out her profession of faith in our love. And she did so to the rhythm of the train...

*"I know my Mommy and Daddy love me! No matter what!*
*I know my Mommy and Daddy love me! No matter what!*
*I know my Mommy and Daddy love me! No matter what!"*

Erin was absolutely convinced that there was nothing ...nor would there ever be anything that could ever change the love we – her Mommy and Daddy – had for her. *No matter what.* And by this unflinching trust in her heart...and to the rhythm of the train...for those three long, *embedding-this-reality-in-my-mind* hours, I was completely humbled, challenged and encouraged, once again, to always and more fully trust in the love of my God.

I am frail, flawed and finite. But here was my little Erin, unabashedly convinced that my love and her Daddy's love for her would never be weak, wounded or wear out. *No matter what.* I had to ask myself: *Do I trust my God and my God's love for me every day in every circumstance? In this same fully uncovered, no-limitations-considered kind of way that my little Erin expressed about our love for her?*

I need to. Each and every day. Because the truth from the very heart of God – from the very heart of my Heavenly Father, my Eternal Abba – *is* that I am loved...I am loved *no matter what.* I am loved by my God.

And it is this powerful, unfailing, unchanging, life-giving, life-healing love of God that changes me from being a victim – a child once horribly bruised and crippled emotionally, mentally, relationally, sexually and spiritually – into being a woman who is *more than a conqueror* through my Lord Jesus Christ who loves me.

*No matter what.*

I am loved by my God. And nothing can or ever will change that I have been loved by my God even before my birth…even when I was treated hatefully…even when I hated viciously. I am loved by my God…even when circumstances are completely out of my control…even when I try to take control and do things in my own frail, flawed and finite way.

I am loved by my God. And His love, which never changes, has changed – and is still changing – everything in me and for me. *No matter what.*

**For I am convinced that neither death nor life, neither angels nor demons, neither the present nor the future, nor any powers, neither height nor depth, nor anything else in all creation will be able to separate us from the love of God that is in Christ Jesus our Lord.**

Romans 8:38-39

I am absolutely, unchangingly, fabulously and foolishly *convinced* that there is nothing at all – not anything from anyone…nothing from my past…nothing now…nothing ever – that will be able to separate me from the love of my God that I have in, and from, my Lord Jesus Christ.

*No matter what.*

And way back in that bathroom during my first year of marriage, God *convinced* me of this – in my mind, my heart and my soul. And this, being *convinced* of God's love, was the powerful weapon that broke open – ever more revealingly – the unhealed and twisted patterns of my thinking, perceiving and doing that had grown out of all those years of evil abuse, cruel hurt and deep rejection.

It was time for God to dig even deeper into my head, heart and spirit in order to root out and cut away every single thought and behavior pattern that held me captive in any way. Freedom and healing was coming to me in layers – coming incrementally – as God ripped away layer after layer of my unhealthy, unholy thought and behavior patterns. As I trusted God's love for me. As I allowed God to make me *more than a conqueror* in Christ – through His passionate and healing love. And as a perfectly loved child of God, I had to allow God to strip away every layer of bondage that was in me – wherever my thought and behavior patterns were insecure...or fearful...or defensive ...or offensive...or prideful...or masked...or hidden...or selfish...or depressed...or angry...or mean...or malicious ...or manipulative...or weak...or worried...or...

*No matter what.*

*No matter* that it would take years of God's Spirit of grace and truth continually reaching out to Mom and Dad, My Sister and My Brothers before they would come to know the transforming love and power of Jesus for themselves. And each one...each one *would* come...and each one *did* come to accept the salvation that Jesus Christ alone offers. God drew each one of them to Himself. I just got to go along for the ride through praying for them and loving on them. (And driving them all a little bit nuts!) But! It was always and only *God's* unfailing mercy and love – just as it was for me – that brought each one of them to salvation.

*Thank You, my God, Thank You! Thank You, my Jesus!*

As for My Sister and My Brothers, their salvation stories are their own – as are their ongoing, continually unfolding, transformation journeys with the Lord Jesus Christ. And these stories are *theirs* for the telling. Not mine. Not here.

I will just celebrate the incredible joy of knowing that *no matter what* our paths here on earth are, we will all be spending eternity with each other and with our Loving, Holy Lord Jesus Christ. He has gone before us to prepare our heavenly homes. And I'm pretty sure we won't be sleeping five to a bunk bed...in a trailer. But even if we did, it would be just fine with me! Because we will all be together – My Big Sister, My Oldest Brother, My Big Brother, My Little Brother and I will all be together – without any ugliness or awkwardness, without any jealousy or pain, without any bitterness or blaming. We will all be held in the unfailing, life-transforming *love* of our Lord Jesus Christ. Forever. Together. I am *convinced.*

And I am *convinced* that it is the love of Jesus that is, right now, holding onto our Mom as well.

On April 29, 1992, Mom went into the hospital to have emergency surgery on what was first thought to be a large blockage in her colon. Forty-one days – two more surgeries, two rounds of chemo and a constant, chaotic roller coaster ride of emotional and physical pain and crises – later, Mom died from what was found to be ovarian cancer. Cancer that had already metastasized throughout all of her major organs, her brain and her blood. And as horrible and tragic as it was, it was never beyond the reach ...nor the will...nor the love of Jesus Christ. Not for one moment. Not ever.

God just needed to get Mom, my very stubborn, prideful, intelligent – and completely mortal – Mom on her back long enough...to quiet her fully enough...to get her to be humble enough...so that Mom could finally face the *truth* of how absolutely desperately she needed the love of Jesus...and His full forgiveness of her most ugly and hidden sins…and His free gift of eternal life that Jesus *alone* could offer her.

As we gathered in the surgical waiting room on that April day in 1992, it was the very first time that My Big Sister, My Big Brother, My Little Brother and I were all together with each of us now living as believers in Jesus Christ. All of us by then had *gotten* God's love and had said, "*Yes*," to the salvation of Jesus. All of us, at that moment in time, were choosing to walk our faith journeys and our lives with Jesus in the lead. And all of us knew that God had brought us together – *for such a time as this* – to share the love, grace, truth and salvation of Jesus Christ with our Mom.

For the first time ever, we were far more than siblings; we were now truly Brothers and Sisters in Jesus. And for that period of time, we were sharing the most beautiful of all relationships. We each knew that God had worked this out for us and for our own relational healing so that we could all be in this *together*. So that we could all be present for and supportive of Mom…and each other. We openly talked about it. And, together, we openly prayed about it.

The fact that Mom had *not* died previously from a heart attack or a stroke – even though she had already suffered from one or more of each of these – was in itself a miracle. So, on April 29, 1992, although we didn't know *how much time* God was going to give to Mom, we each recognized that God had given Mom *this time* – this generous gift of time for Mom to face her own mortality and her need for Jesus.

Mom was brave outwardly *even while* she was terrified inwardly. She was a composed, professional woman *and* she was a frantic, angry child. Mom was proud and stubborn *and* she had been brought low and forced to see the fragility of her life and the shame of her sins. *Because God loved her so much.*

This generous gift of time was God's way of lovingly, mercifully, passionately *opening a window* for Mom – giving her the opportunity to know and accept for herself the merciful, eternal salvation offered through Jesus – even as God was firmly, and with complete finality, *closing the door* to her mortal life here on earth.

And for Mom, God pulled out all the stops. Because God's like that. God's love knows no bounds. *No matter what.*

Mom was surrounded with us – her four, living Christian children – who were even stronger and bolder in sharing our faith because, right then, we also had each other. And we were all there, almost every single day, caring for Mom. Visiting her, calming her, laughing with her, washing her, spending nights with her – and telling her that she needed to know and trust the love and salvation of Jesus.

And Mom would ask me, as she did when My Oldest Brother died eleven years earlier, to pick out some Scripture verses *for* her. But now, in her pain and in her need, Mom asked me to read those Scripture passages out loud *to* her. Mom would also ask me to sing to her while she lay on her back – out of control of her body, out of control of her life.

And I sang a lot over those six weeks.

One of her favorite, and most often requested, songs for me to sing was the old hymn, "In The Garden." Mom loved the outdoors and she loved roses, especially yellow roses. And so, with Mom's eyes closed as I sang, my soul would be singing and praying that Mom, in her spirit, would be walking with Jesus, right then, in a beautiful and quiet garden filled with magnificent flowers and trees and an extra abundance of perfectly formed and fragrant yellow roses.

When I came to the chorus, Mom's face would become a little less tense – a little less angry, a little less prideful, a little less pained – and Mom's breath would become a little more calm, a little more steady, a little more deep, a little more peaceful. And every once in awhile, Mom (even with her not-for-public-singing-voice) would join with me as I sang the chorus of "In The Garden" to her:

*I come to the garden alone*
*while the dew is still on the roses,*
*and the voice I hear falling on my ear,*
*the Son of God discloses.*
*And He walks with me, and He talks with me,*
*and He tells me I am His own;*
*and the joy we share as we tarry there,*
*none other has ever known.*[1]

And I sang with my voice, my heart, my soul and every longing within me for Mom to know Jesus. For Mom to fully, and for all eternity, know and accept Jesus and His passionate, perfect love for her. And I prayed that as I sang, Mom would hear God telling her…

> **The LORD your God is with you,**
> **He is mighty to save.**
> **He will take great delight in you,**
> **He will quiet you with His love,**
> **He will rejoice over you with singing.**
> Zephaniah 3:17

These were such intimate times. Times to just be with Mom. Just love on Mom. I had already forgiven Mom years and years ago, so there was no unfinished business for me. Mom never admitted to me any of the pain she had caused or any of the abuse she had allowed to happen. But *that* didn't matter. It wasn't to me that Mom had to confess. Mom never asked for my forgiveness, for anything. It wasn't from me that Mom needed to receive forgiveness.

Our time spent together was all and only about loving on Mom with the love that God had given me. For the most part, God had me just stay very quiet with Mom – still always sharing the salvation Jesus offered to her and, yet, always sharing this bold message with a deep gentleness and tenderness. Much of my time with Mom was spent calming her anger that sometimes went out of control and into hysteria because of the medications she was on or because her Valium had been taken away from her far too quickly or because of all the physical-emotional-spiritual-pain she was feeling. My time with Mom was also spent washing her face, her feet and her bum...drying her tears and cooling her forehead...shaving her legs and brushing her hair...fluffing her pillows and re-tucking her sheets ...and always reading, singing and praying...and always trusting that God would bring Mom home to Him.

Sadly, Dad was not – could not be...would not be – really present for Mom on so many levels. Dad would be wandering in the hospital halls or sitting in the lounge or in the hospital cafeteria or by Mom's bedside for only brief periods of time...at a time, Dad often seemed overwhelmed by the outrageous reality of Mom's imminent death – of Mom needing to be the center of attention in such intense ways. Attention given to her by medical professionals, co-workers, friends and her children. Dad was still horribly trapped in his own very unwell place. He often seemed shell-shocked, numb or numbed by his pills and his drinking. He still acted in some very selfish and narcissistic ways. I know that Dad loved Mom – even idolized her in some ways, finding much of his own pride and identity in Mom's public persona and accomplishments. I know that Dad loved Mom. But their twisted, needy, co-dependent, *antinomy-filled* life as a married couple was coming to an end. And Dad was lost...and helpless...and often very unhelpful.

From the very first surgery, God just opened the doors wide for Mom to be surrounded with many loving, believing Christians. Mom was *surrounded by a great cloud of witnesses* (Hebrews 12:1) that went far beyond her four, living Christian children – and was in no way limited by Dad's limitations to be present for Mom in her suffering and dying.

And for Mom, God pulled out all the stops. Because God's like that. God's love knows no bounds. *No matter what.*

Mom's Anesthesiologist was an extremely intelligent (like Mom), big, bold, Jesus-loving (not like Mom) woman, who just happened to be married to the Jesus-loving, truth-telling, compassionate, funny and ever-available Hospital Chaplain! Both spent so much time with Mom. Loving her. Telling Mom about the loving truth of Jesus that they both knew deeply for themselves...and that they wanted her to know too.

Mom's Respiratory Therapist was the mother of a high school friend of mine who, when her husband was fighting his battle with cancer, had invited me, even as a teenager, to come up to the hospital to pray with him and to pray with her whole family. This precious woman had seen the love of Jesus in me, and my faith in God's compassionate heart. And she wanted me to share that with her, her husband and her family. It was an incredibly humbling time for me to be so intimately invited into someone else's life. Invited to be present in her husband's dying process. And to face, with them, his death through which he entered into eternal life with Jesus. And now, *here* was this beautiful, faith-filled mother of my high school friend sharing intimately and boldly with Mom. Telling her of Jesus. Giving Mom hope and bringing her comfort.

Then, our God – whose love knows no bounds – brought to Mom a Head Nurse who Mom had known for a very long time…a Head Nurse who knew Jesus intimately…and a Head Nurse whom Mom had actually helped to get out of her own destructive marriage to an alcoholic, drug-using, abusive man. *Now* it was this Head Nurse's time to minister to Mom. Minister to Mom in her many desperate, physical needs. And far beyond that, this Head Nurse was there to minister to Mom with the life-transforming love, healing and salvation of our Lord Jesus Christ.

This Head Nurse was my Becky.

And for Mom, God pulled out all the stops. Because God's like that. God's love knows no bounds. *No matter what.*

*God's great cloud of witnesses* – My Big Sister, My Big Brother, My Little Brother and I…and all of our families …Mom's Anesthesiologist, Hospital Chaplain, Respiratory Therapist and Mom's Head Nurse – my Becky, along with so many other hospital staff members, co-workers and friends from the church – *surrounded* Mom during this gift of time that God had given to her. And we loved on Mom, cared for her, listened to her, shared with her, read and sang to her and prayed for Mom to accept the forgiveness and the salvation of Jesus.

And Mom did.

Three days before she died, the Hospital Chaplain told us simply that Mom had accepted the love and forgiveness of Jesus – Mom had put her faith in Jesus as her Savior. It was not his to disclose anything that Mom had shared in confidentiality with him. It was not his to tell us what Mom had confessed that needed the forgiveness of Jesus. It didn't matter. Mom had yielded to the humbling and outrageous, passionate and persistent love of our Holy God that placed Jesus on the cross. And in His love Mom crossed over from the realm of mortality to immortality and accepted her promised place in heaven.

I cannot even begin to fathom the spiritual battle that had to be going on inside of Mom's head and spirit – because of all the things she had done…because of all the things she didn't do – even as her body was being destroyed by cancer. But God knew. And God won.

For those last three days of Mom's life on earth, a dove sat on the ledge outside Mom's hospital window. All day. All night. For all of those three days. I believe it was God's unimaginable kindness that placed that dove there as a sign for Mom to know that the promise of eternal life through the sacrifice and resurrection of Jesus – this promise in which she had just placed her trust – was a sure promise and secure hope.

Mom also recognized that this dove *was* God's sign of His love for her. She knew that God had placed that dove on her hospital room window ledge – all day, all night, for all those three days – as a messenger of the peace and hope of Jesus. When I went to visit Mom on her last day on earth, I brought with me My *Almost-Thirteen-Year-Old* Niece – Mom's Granddaughter...the Daughter of My *Already-Gone-To-Jesus* Oldest Brother.

This was the first time in a long time that Mom and My Niece had seen each other. In the face of My Niece, Mom got to see My Oldest Brother – Her Oldest Son. And for a flicker of time, I could sense the spiritual battle of sin and shame that was raising its ugly head against the truth of God's love and mercy within Mom's heart and head – the spiritual battle of death and life was suddenly heightened, once again, and was fiercely intense for Mom – for a moment...when she first saw her Granddaughter...the Daughter of Her Oldest Son.

The dove cooed. And God won. Again. For all eternity.

Although Mom's eyes were covered by that nearly-blinded-death-glaze that often comes over the eyes of those whose death is imminent, Mom looked over to that God-placed dove sitting on her hospital room window ledge. And the dove cooed again, and the dove reassured Mom that the battle was over. God had won. And nothing in all creation – nothing that Mom had ever done...and nothing that Mom had ever failed to do – would ever be able to separate her from the love of God that is in Christ Jesus our Lord. And Mom was *convinced* of this.

And Mom calmed. And she breathed a little more deeply. And she smiled. She looked over once again at the dove, and without taking her eyes off the dove, Mom told us that she knew Jesus had placed it there for *her* so that she would know that He would lead her home. And Mom smiled. She was at peace. Mom was *convinced* of God's love, forgiveness and promise of eternal life.

My Niece and I had stayed with Mom for as long as we possibly could that day. I needed to drive us back to Fairport, New York, about a two hour trip from room 426 at the Oswego Hospital. Because we had to get back home in time to attend my Julia's end-of-the-school-year program. Julia was going to be in her kindergarten class' Nursery Rhyme Pageant playing a lead role as *Mary, Mary Quite Contrary* – all decked out in her fluffy dress, little white bonnet and wielding a plastic, red and yellow watering can. And I, Julia's Mommy, needed to be there for My Baby Girl.

I kissed and hugged Mom goodbye. She was sitting up in her hospital room's not-so-comfortable easy chair. I told Mom how thankful I was that we would be spending eternity together...with Jesus...and her dove. I told Mom I loved her so much. She told me she loved me too. I held her hands and prayed with Mom one last time. We hugged again and squeezed hands. And I saw that Mom's big, round blue eyes – although they were almost entirely blind to this world – were at peace. Mom smiled and waved a little wave as we walked out of room 426.

Leaving, the tears started rolling down my face. No sobs. Just tears. I was pretty sure this would be the last time I would see Mom on this earth. I couldn't talk. I was so overwhelmed by the mercy of God and His love for Mom ...for me...for all of His children – from which we can never be separated. And I knew that Mom was God's child. And that my prayer – and my letter for us to never be eternally separated – had been passionately, perfectly answered by the love of God that knows no bounds. The love of God that just needs to be believed and received by us.

Mom had believed…Mom had received God's love.

And later on that June 10, 1992 night – after our little kindergarten actress Julia, our Erin and our Niece were all tucked into bed after *Prayers and Thankfuls* – I got a phone call from My Big Sister. She and My Little Brother had been with Mom in her last moments. Mom had asked My Big Sister to turn off, just for a moment, the machine attached to her nasal-gastric tube. Mom wanted *just one more taste* of TaB – her favorite diet soda. That was just like Mom. And I'm sure Mom asked for it with a wink in her glazed-over eyes and a feeling of victory as she bucked the chains of hospital protocol off from her…and took *just one more* big, yummy swig of her TaB. My Big Sister and My Little Brother had actually just left Mom's room for the evening and had to be called back when, with God's loving hands reaching out to her, Mom bucked the chains of this earth off from her – all the chains of sickness, sin, pain, abuse and death. Mom and her dove went home with Jesus.

*Thank You, my God, Thank You! Thank You, my Jesus!*

# *11*

## *Do not conform any longer to the pattern of this world, but be transformed by the renewing of your mind.*
*Romans 12:2*

After Mom's death, *after Mom's entry into her eternal life with Jesus*, it would be more than ten...long... years of loving on Dad with prayers, tears, talking, silence, writing, calling, visiting, dealing with Dad's meanness towards me and Dad's rejection of me. And it would be more than ten...long...years of God orchestrating an intense *Jeremiah-burning-in-my-heart-and-in-my-bones-call-from-God* period when I knew God was telling me to continually share, clearly and specifically, the gospel of Jesus Christ with Dad...before Dad would come to the place of humility and sincere recognition of his own desperate need for the love and salvation of Jesus Christ.

My head still spins a bit when I think of the intensity of so many of those times I spent with Dad. And my heart is still awed and humbled by the unfailing power of the inseparable love of God.

*No matter what.*

Being *convinced* of God's unchanging love changes – and *still is* changing – everything in me.

God's transforming, healing, strength-bringing, grace-offering, truth-bearing, freedom-declaring work of *love*, all starts in the greatest of all battlefields: Our Minds.

***Do not conform any longer to the pattern of this world,***
***but be transformed by the renewing of your mind...***
Romans 12:2

Trusting, truly trusting in God's love for me, and the truth that Jesus would never let go of His hold on me, is what made it possible for me to choose to *not conform any longer to the pattern of this world, but be transformed by the renewing of my mind.*

Jesus would uncover and show me – lovingly, sternly, compassionately and continuously – every way that my patterns of thinking, speaking and acting didn't line up with *God's truth:* That through the love of Jesus I am *more than a conqueror.* And, oh my! There were a lot of twisted patterns over a lot of years for Jesus to uncover and show me!

And the show isn't over! Jesus is *so* not done with me yet! I am still, and will always remain, in the construction ...reconstruction...*transformation* zone while I live on this side of heaven. Because the patterns of this world are oh-so-very-different from the patterns of minds renewed through God's loving work of transformation.

God's love makes all the difference. All the renewing, life-transforming difference.

The pattern of this world's thinking would have *understood* if I had committed suicide after being raped by The Passenger. There would have been some shock. Some sadness. But the pattern of this world's thinking would have *understood* why I chose this final and extreme way out of my pain. The pattern of this world could only see a little girl so bruised and so damaged that my suicide would have been absolutely *understandable.* Maybe even expected. This world's pattern of thinking would have concluded that my suicide was probably the only way out for me to truly escape from the repercussions of such horrendous victimization. This world's pattern of thinking probably would have concluded that: *At least one more abused child would finally be at rest. We understand why she did it.* (There may have even been a sigh of relief going out from the crowd.)

But following and acting in accordance with the pattern of this world's thinking does not – could not – bring me a life-transforming difference. It only brings me death.

The pattern of this world's thinking would have *understood* if the next time Dad had approached me – to hurt me, to touch me, to rape me – I had taken one of his guns and blown his head off. The pattern of this world's thinking would have *understood* if I had killed Dad. There would have been some shock. Some sadness. But the pattern of this world's thinking would have *understood* why I chose this final and extreme way out of my pain. The pattern of this world could only see a little girl so bruised and so damaged that murdering Dad would have been absolutely *understandable.* Maybe even expected. This world's pattern of thinking would have concluded that murdering Dad was probably the only way out for me to truly escape from the repercussions of such horrendous victimization. This world's pattern of thinking probably would have concluded that: *At least one more child rapist would finally be gone from the face of this earth and could never hurt anyone else, ever again. We understand why she did it.* (There may have even been a cheer of satisfaction going up from the crowd.)

But following and acting in accordance with the pattern of this world's thinking does not – could not – bring me a life-transforming difference. It only brings me death.

God's loving, mind-and-life-transforming ways are not always (and most often are not) *understandable* to people who are, sadly, still trapped in their thinking by the patterns of this world. God's ultimate, loving, mind and life-transforming plan for me, and for *all* of God's children who place their faith in Jesus Christ as Savior, is:

### *...to be conformed in the likeness of His Son...*
Romans 8:29

And for me, as Jesus lovingly, sternly, compassionately and continuously worked to transform me...and to shape me to be more like Him, it meant I had to completely *yield* my bruised and twisted patterns of thinking, speaking and acting, over and over and over again, to line up with *God's truth:* That through the love of Jesus I am more than a conqueror.

And as more than a conqueror and as a yielded *bucket* to the love and power of Jesus (because I just can't do it on my own!) that renews and transforms my mind and my life:

I choose life instead of death.
I choose love instead of hate.
I choose forgiveness instead of bitterness.
I choose mercy instead of vengeance.
I choose compassion instead of coldness.
I choose peace instead of panic.
I choose courage instead of fear.
I choose trust instead of doubt.

I choose strength instead of weakness.

I choose thankfulness instead of self-pity.

I choose humility instead of pride.

I choose vulnerable dependence on Jesus instead of self-protective, prideful independence.

I choose and celebrate God's good, loving and freeing gift of sexuality for Tim and me instead of being held captive to a warped view of sexuality that would see it only as evil, ugly, selfish, manipulative and hurtful.

I choose freedom in Christ instead of bondage to anything or anyone else.

I choose to believe that *nothing in all creation will be able to separate me from the love of God that is in Christ Jesus my Lord!*

*No matter what!*

After Mom's death, *after Mom's entry into her eternal life with Jesus*, it would be, for Dad, more than ten...long...years...of mind-numbing loss, depression, drunkenness, addiction, prescription forgery for his narcotics, anger, cruelty, abuse, outrageous lies, several medical emergencies and surgeries, physical and emotional trauma and at least three more women in his life.

God doesn't change. And God's call on my life didn't change. God had called me to be in, and stay in, Dad's life – with the powerful truth of God's inseparable love and by continually yielding to God's transforming and renewing of my mind...over and over and over again!

The first woman in Dad's life, after Mom went home to Jesus, was Mary. She was nice, yet fairly quiet. So, I never felt like I knew Mary all that well or knew much of anything about her. Mary became Dad's live-in girlfriend within just a couple of months after Mom died. Christmas of 1992, Dad and Mary were just two of the twenty-two people (and a puppy) that we invited to stay overnight at our home in Fairport, New York, for our family's first Christmas after Mom died. As a family of this size, we had never all stayed overnight together in the same place with all of our spouses, children, one puppy *and* Grandpa Lodge too. (It was only a little more than a month before Grandpa died in February 1993.)

I know I didn't win any points with Dad when I explained (albeit very gently) that he and Mary would have to sleep in separate beds. Only the married couples got the double beds in our house. At that moment, Dad surprisingly did as he did when I told him I would walk myself down the aisle when I married Tim. Dad calmly accepted the boundaries I set and respected my decision. *Okay! Head spin!* Dad and Mary could have gone to a hotel, but they chose to stay and seemed to be glad that they did. And Mary and Dad were both welcomed. The two of them seemed so needy...and they seemed to fill a need for each other...at least at that time...for a short time.

That Christmas of 1992, there was no crazy pressure to share extravagant presents. Just simple gifts were given to the children. This was a time to share lots of food and fun with each other and enjoy having all our children together – ranging in age from fourteen to three years – playing together with all their cousins and with that crazy, hyperactive puppy, rightly named Lightning (*my-once-upon-a-time-nickname*). Early on Christmas morning, Tim read the story of the birth of Jesus to all twenty-two of us (and the puppy) as we gathered in our living room. Tim read about God's love gift of Jesus from Luke, Chapter Two. And he read it aloud from that gigantic, red, *family*

Bible with its fancy, gold, scripted letters of *Holy Bible* on the cover. That Bible, which had belonged to Mom's grandparents and had brought me comfort when terrorized, was now in our home and being read from for all my family to hear.

*Wow, God.*

Not too long after that Christmas, Mary and Dad just seemed to drift apart. They had enjoyed each other's company for a time, but, apparently, their connection just didn't have the makings for a long-term relationship. Dad's only commentary about this was, *"Well, we jus' went our sep'rit ways after awhile. No hard feelin's b'tween us. I guess it jus' wuzn't meant to be."*

The second woman in Dad's life, after Mom died, was Elli. Dad married Elli in August 1994. I liked her, although I wouldn't want her to be ticked off at me. She was a tough, first generation, big German woman – and I thought she might be just the kind of don't-mess-with-me-woman that Dad could use to help *straighten him out*. And maybe, with Elli in Dad's life, that might mean that I would be able to back out of the picture a bit more with Dad.

Nope. That wasn't God's plan. Doggone it! About a month before Dad and Elli got married, God had put me in another one of His *Jeremiah-burning-in-my-heart-and-in-my-bones-call-from-God* modes. After a time of fasting, praying and staying up for one entire night wrestling with God (Because I didn't like what I was being told to do. Doggone it!), I knew that God had called me to tell Elli of Dad's abusive behavior – of which, it appeared, she was either unconcerned or unaware.

The spiritual battle was fierce. The enemy of God battered me with lies, accusing me of only wanting to tell

Elli about Dad's past because I had never really forgiven Dad...and that I didn't want Dad to have any happiness in his future. These were lies. But the battle was intense. I had to dig deep into my soul...I had to invite God into my innermost being to completely sort out my every motive, my every thought, my every word, my every action. It was grueling. Trying. Emotional. Tiring. *Freeing.*

God won. God's love and grace and truth won. And I submitted.

I knew after all the wrestling with God (and because of the absolute truth that *I did not want to do this*...at all!) that talking to Elli really was *not* about me. It was all about God. It was all about God wanting to show His love to Elli. My call was to present God's love and truth to Elli – and to give Elli the knowledge she needed to have in order to make a decision about her relationship with Dad. God's demanding call on my life was also about cleaning me out more and more so that I could – through God's love – offer honest, stripped-down, self-sacrificing love to Dad. Because neither God nor I wanted him to continue in his destructive patterns. There was nothing in me that *wanted* to do this. Nothing. Yet, everything in me knew that I would have absolutely no peace until I trusted and obeyed God with His most recent, bizarre call on my life. With this specific and purposeful and unrelenting *Jeremiah-burning-in-my-heart-and-in-my-bones-call-from-God.*

*Okay, God.*

Elli and I met at a restaurant. I prayed before we ate our meal. I prayed for God's love and truth to be made known and God's peace to hold us together. (And silently I prayed that I wouldn't throw up!) I started our conversation by letting Elli know that anything and everything I said, she could repeat to Dad. I told her that I loved Dad. That I wanted him happy, whole and at peace with God. I wanted her to know that everything she would learn of Dad's behavior in our family had all already been forgiven...and all of it had been spoken (or written) to Dad years ago.

And so, with a very sick stomach (Because I still didn't want to do this! Doggone it!), yet in a very calm and strong voice, and out of a heart of inexplicable love that *only* God could have provided, I told Elli about Dad.

Elli said that Dad had told her that he *"had gotten drunk sumtimes"*...that he *"would git doped up on all his narcotics 'cuz of all the pain he wuz feelin'"*...that he *"could get really mean and ugly"*...and *"do sum hurtful things"*...but he *"didn't really remember too much 'bout those years 'cuz he wuz always in so much pain"*...or he *"wuz so rum-dumb because of the booze and dope."* Dad had told Elli that he *"wuzn't drinkin' no mo', 'cept maybe jus' a glass or two onst in awhile"*...and now Dad had his *"dope all under control...things were dif'rent now."* And Elli believed that Dad was different now. (Well, good!)

Elli didn't seem shocked by anything I told her. Nor did she really respond. (*I wondered if Elli ever played poker. I bet she'd be good at it.*) Elli had only a couple of questions to ask me, *"If all this happened, how could you still have a relationship with your father? How could you bring your children to see him?"*

Good questions.

I shared with Elli about the love and forgiveness of Jesus Christ that had completely changed my heart, my life...and twirled me around to live in freedom, courage, mercy and love.

*And* I told Elli that, *"Being loving and forgiving doesn't mean that I'm stupid, naive or a door mat. I still have to be very wise and cautious in all my interactions with Dad. For example, while Mom was dying and after she died, there were many times that I stayed overnight at Dad's house to help him out. But on those nights, I always slept with the door locked and with me fully clothed and my suitcase, shoes and keys set out, ready for me to grab them and run out the door the instant I sensed any danger coming from Dad. And as a Mommy to my Erin and Julia – and in order to set wise and protective boundaries for our babies – Tim and I had put it in our wills, as soon as Erin was born (and even before I could drive after my C-section), and long before Mom died, that if Tim and I were to die while our children were still minors, they were never to be alone with Dad and/or Mom. Never. We still wanted our children to have a relationship with my parents – but only under the very specific, supervised-visitation guidelines that we set up. God's love and forgiveness are powerful, healing and life-transforming! And choosing to live out our lives in love and forgiveness towards Dad does not mean that I should ever be foolish enough to put my own beautiful babies in a potentially destructive and abusive situation. That would not be love."*

By this information alone, did Elli seem to be especially moved as to the depth and reality of all the things that I had shared with her. Generally, however, Elli expressed that she felt quite confident that Dad was a very different man than he may have been years before…and certainly *she* was a very different woman than was My Mother. (*Oh, Pride!*)

I told Elli that I really hoped and prayed that Dad's life was healed…that he really had changed…that Dad and Elli would let God hold and lead them both…and that the two of them would be happy together. I just wanted Elli to pray and seek God's wisdom in all of this.

Dad called me just two days after I met with Elli. He started the conversation with, *"Girl! I've gotta bone to pick with you!"* Dad, then, went off on me with a tirade of *"How dare you tell Elli that you put in your will that your babies could never be alone with us! Who the hell do you think you are? You had jus' better know right here an' now that I don't never wants you to ever be telling me or Elli anything mo' 'bout God! Never agin! If you were the goddamn good little Christian that you pretend to be you wouldn't never do nothing' like that! I am your father! How could you hurt me so bad? So, girl! What the hell you gotta say fo' yourself an' your goddamn holier-than-thou-attitude now?"*

God was with me. And although I felt like I just wanted to run away…or, yes, throw up, I did neither. To Dad, and by that twirling around power of God's love, when life makes me absolutely dizzy, I answered him in a calm voice, a heart of love…and some hard-hitting truth.

*"Dad, I told Elli she could tell you everything I said because I love you. I forgive you. I have nothing to hide. And I want God's best for you. And, Yes, I know you are my father. And only because of that, have Tim and I made the decision – because of God's love – to stay in relationship with you…and let our girls know you as their Grandpa… and have a relationship with you. On our terms. Listen, Dad, I want you to seriously think about this: Do you really think that there would ever be any reason for – or any way that – I would ever allow my two beautiful baby girls to*

ever have any kind of a relationship with any other known child rapist?!"

Dad was silent. I kept going. Still gently, yet strongly.

*"Dad, think about that. It would be wrong and horribly foolish of me to put my girls into such an evil and risky relationship with a known child rapist. Dad, it is only because you are my father that I am allowing and inviting you to be in our girls' lives in any way whatsoever. So, Dad, before you keep going off on me, think about this seriously. I love you. I forgive you. And you need to understand that my first responsibility is to my family – and to love and protect my babies in the very best way that I know how. And for now, that means setting up those loving, righteous, protective boundaries for them. I do want my girls to know you, Dad. And yet it will have to be on our terms. And those are terms that come from God's own love and protection for His babies."*

Silence, now. On both our parts.

I took a deep breath and closed our conversation. *"I love you, Dad. God bless you."*

Very quietly, with no more anger or indignation in his voice (and I believe with some cutting into him by God's truth – and some shock at God's mercy), Dad closed the conversation simply. *"Aw-right, Laney. 'Bye."*

And, once again, the Word of God was reassuring me of God's unfailing, inseparable love...and His Spirit was calming and strengthening me. The Word of God was transforming and renewing my mind so that I could walk... and talk...and act...in ways that had *nothing* to do with the pattern of this world and *everything* to do with God's counter-intuitive ways.

*For I am convinced that...nothing in all creation is able*
*to separate us from the love of God*
*that is in Christ Jesus our Lord.*
Romans 8: 37-39

**Do not conform any longer to the pattern of this world,**
**but be transformed by the renewing of your minds...**
Romans 12:2

*Thank You, God. (Can I have a vacation now???)*

Dad and Elli were married in August 1994. Their marriage ended in divorce after Elli had Dad committed to Benjamin Rush, a psychiatric hospital in Syracuse, New York, in early June 1995 for abuse, holding her hostage and attempting to murder her. This outrageous episode ended with yet another shoot-out with the police. After Elli called me to let me know what happened and where Dad was, we only spoke one more time after that ugly and brutal experience. Elli removed herself from Dad's life quickly and completely. And from mine as well. I pray that Elli has healed from all that she went through...and that she knows the love, peace, hope and life that only Jesus can give.

With Dad being committed (though only for a few weeks) to Benjamin Rush, our family had a great opportunity, albeit a very difficult and emotional one, that we never had before. My Big Sister and I requested a family intervention meeting with Dad under the supervision of his psychiatrist and other appropriate staff members at the psychiatric hospital. So, in mid June 1995, My Big Sister, My Big Brother, My Little Brother and I sat with Dad in a big circle...in a big room...to confront Dad with the destructiveness of his behavior towards all of us – including towards Mom and My Oldest Brother – and towards himself. We were there to confront Dad with his need to get help. And to help move him to take advantage of this time to finally get the help and healing he needed.

And we confronted Dad with love. Even in our pain. Our shame. Our frustration. And our desperately wanting something very different for Dad and for all of us. There were tears from all of us. No one hated Dad. Just hated what he had done to us. And the hateful way he had treated us. My Big Sister, My Big Brother, My Little Brother and I spoke things that, until that point in time, had never been spoken out loud for all of us to hear and know.

From My Big Sister came deep hurt, anguish of soul and self-suffocating anger. Dad had scarred her deeply, emotionally and sexually, and she wasn't over it yet. How could he have done all that he did to her? How could she be his *Princess*, as he often called her, and be so used and abused by him? How could Dad say that he loved her when he treated her in such shameful and evil ways?

From My Little Brother came heartbreaking, shameful, embarrassing, angry stories birthed from the consequences of Dad's cruelty and abuse which continued against him when he was the only one of the five children still living at home – the evil and sick abuse that My Little Brother suffered alone after the rest of us had graduated from high school and moved out.

From me, I told my story too. And I reminded Dad of the letter I wrote years ago. The letter that, until then, My Sister and My Brothers did not know I had written. The letter in which I called abuse *abuse* and incest *incest* and gave Mom and Dad my full forgiveness and desperately pleaded with them to accept the love and salvation of Jesus because I did not want to be eternally separated from them.

I told Dad that I had no unfinished business with him for myself. I just wanted him to get help. I wanted the drama and the brokenness to stop. Now. I wanted Dad to stop drinking and getting all doped up on his meds. I wanted Dad to stop causing so much pain in the lives of those that were most closely involved with him. I wanted the evil choices Dad was making to stop. I wanted Dad to choose God's forgiveness, salvation and new life. Now.

From My Big Brother came mostly a stunned surprise, some shaking of his head and a confused look on his face as he listened to each of us speak our strong truths about the abuse and incest we had suffered at Dad's hands. *"Did I grow up in a different family? In a different home? Where was I? How could all of this have been happening and I didn't know about it? I know Dad did a lot of stupid, mean things. But I never knew it was this bad. But, whatever. It's over now. We just have to live our lives and move on. We all made it through. It's all done. The past is past. We just have to enjoy life and stop looking back."*

My Big Brother's stunned response, to the truth being exposed by My Big Sister, My Little Brother and me, left me in my own state of disbelief and surprise. *Wow.* So many thoughts were going through my head – I wondered how he had been so mentally protected (or so deeply entrenched in denial) that his reality and perceptions were so very different from mine and from the rest of us. On one level I was so happy for My Big Brother. On another level I was deeply concerned.

*No matter what…*I knew I had to trust God's heart and God's grace and truth for My Big Brother…and for every member of my family…and for me. God's love and healing come to all of us who seek Jesus. And yet, sometimes

God's love and healing come to different people in very different ways and at very different times...and sometimes at very different levels of intensity and revelation...and sometimes at very different, even mysterious, mind-renewing, life-transforming kinds of ways.

For the most part, during this intervention session, Dad was pretty quiet. When he did speak, his focus was on defending himself, though not in an offensive way. Dad just didn't seem to remember doing the things we told him he had done to us. He had been drunk. He had been doped up. He was in so much physical pain. He had gone through so much in his own life. So much hell and hurt from his own growing up. No one had ever really loved him except Vivian (Mom). There were tears when Dad said that.

And then, the criticism began. Dad had some for each of us. Dad's attacks to *and* about me were: "*Laney, you's always talkin' 'bout God. Won't never shut up 'bout wantin' things to change an' git better. So damn serious an' intense all the goddamn time. Even as a little kid, Droopy Drawers, you wuz always jus' so damn over-sensitive, 'bout ever' little, itty-bitty, cotton-pickin' thing! You couldn't jus' git over things an' git on with it. An' I am jus' so damn tar'd of all the Jesus talk comin' from you. It is jus' too goddamn much. You jus' gotta stop.*"

I really had to ask God to get *and* keep my head in that tight vise-grip of His love. Right now! I had to immediately *and* determinedly choose – with every ounce of mental, physical and spiritual strength available to me – not to scream...but to choose instead the wisdom of silence...and the willingness to be rejected, misjudged and shut down, once again, by Dad. I had to choose – with every fiber of my being *and* through the love of God – not to reject

Dad...but to choose instead to understand that Dad still was not able, ready, cognizant, willing or remorseful enough to deal directly with the horrendous emotional, physical and sexual abuse that I – and the others – had suffered at his hands. My head was spinning. But God kept me balanced, calm, and quiet in my words and attitude.

At least until I got in my car.

The two hour ride home alone was a time for God to hold me in that unrelenting love vise-grip of His and remind me of the deep, life-transforming truths of His loving grace that *had already* set me free...and that I needed to always keep in mind in order to *stay* free. But the battle was fierce. So fierce, in fact, that I had to pull off on the side of the NY State Thruway between Syracuse and Rochester so that I could just let myself cry out...sob out... scream out...all the heart-wrenching confusion, insanity and sadness that I felt after that family intervention meeting. And I called out to God, from the deepest part of my gut and soul, with my outrageously passionate – and, yes, *serious, intense and, maybe even, over-sensitive* – desire for my *whole family* to get healed...*completely and truly* healed. Right now! Now! Now!

A Policeman pulled over behind me, but I was shaking so much and crying so hard that I never saw him until he knocked on my car door window. Aaaaggghhh! I think I experienced my first heart attack right then and there...or, at least, shortened the time until I would meet Jesus face to face by at least three years!

The Policeman asked, *"Ma'am, are you okay?"* My first (inside of my head) response was, *Duh! What you think? Do I look like I'm okay, Sherlock?*

But thankfully, very thankfully, God's love vise-grip held my mouth tightly enough so that I could answer with far greater composure and maturity than I felt, *"I am. But my Dad is very sick and in the hospital. I just needed to pull over and let myself cry. I'll be okay, now, Officer. Thank you."*

The Policeman was very kind, although I'm pretty sure he did bend a little extra close to smell my breath and look inside my car for any evidence that I may have been drinking. *"Take a few more minutes to get yourself together, Ma'am. But then, you need to continue on your way home. It really isn't safe to pull over on the side of the Thruway."*

I thanked The Policeman, again, and watched as he walked back to his car and spoke into his radio – most likely reporting about the crazy, crying woman on the side of the road. 10-4. Over and Out.

When I finally got home, our eleven year old Erin and nine year old Julia were already asleep. Timmy greeted me with a deep, loving, just-holding-me-quietly-strong hug. I told him I wasn't even going to try to analyze or sort out my tightly knotted, twisted head. I was just going to fall into my Abba's arms and ask my God to do this for me. I wasn't even going to talk about all that had just happened. I just needed to let God's Spirit pray for me, heal me, touch me, unwind me…and remind me of the love, the grace, the truth and the eternal perspective of my Jesus.

As I fell into my bed that night – physically, emotionally and spiritually exhausted – I asked my Abba to come into my head…to do within my head and heart and spirit all that I could not do on my own. And God's Holy Spirit loved on me so intimately, with such tenderness and such power throughout the night. When I woke the next morning, I felt a physical, mental and spiritual peace in my brain and in my spirit that was deeper and calmer than anything I had ever felt before. This peace could not, and *did* not, come from me...not from me figuring any of this out...not from me getting my perspective all back together.

No. This was a deep, intimate gift from God's Spirit who had lovingly, diligently, intricately hugged and massaged my tightly knotted head and heart throughout my sleep that night. God's Holy, Intimate, Care-taking, Loving Holy Spirit had wakened me that next morning with the knowledge that *God* had brought me back to peace and balance. God had brought me back to breathing and hope... to courage and joy...and to a willingness to keep on doing things in God's ways that are counter-intuitive to the pattern of this world.

God had brought me back to trusting Him and His love for me. *No matter what.*

I am God's child. I am God's woman. I am healed. In Christ I am more than a conqueror. I am not a victim in any way...any longer. I am *convinced* that there is nothing – not the most ugly abuse or the most hurtful rejection or denial or misjudgment or criticism or dismissal of my heart and personhood – there is nothing in all creation...in all of my experiences...that will ever be able to separate me from the love of God that is in Christ Jesus my Lord. *I am convinced. And I am transformed and renewed.*

*Thank You, my Abba. Thank You, my Jesus. Thank You, Holy Spirit.*

The next day I spent all my time just thanking my God and loving on my Timmy, my Erin and my Julia...and *being loved on* by them. It was time to just be very present with these precious ones in my life…nothing else mattered …nothing else was more important. We spent most of that beautiful June day outside! Fun and silliness, bike rides and brunch, singing and dancing, playing and laughing…and twirling around…and it was all so good for my soul!

A couple of weeks later, Dad was released from Benjamin Rush Psychiatric Hospital with the *prescription and on condition* that he was to follow up with his local drug rehabilitation center. My Big Sister and I went together to bring Dad back home. Dad was a little quiet, but seemed fairly light-hearted on the drive back. And he was hungry. We stopped at an Olive Garden, one of Dad's favorite places to eat. *Doesn't everybody do that on the way home from a psychiatric hospital?* I asked if it would be okay (being the *Jesus freak* that I am) if we could have a blessing before we ate. Dad answered gently, actually looking at me, *"Yeah, Laney. You do that."* A short blessing…a quick meal…and we were back on the road. I stayed at Dad's house that night – and as I usually did when staying there, I slept with the door locked and with me fully clothed and my suitcase, shoes and keys set out, ready for me to grab them and run out the door the instant I sensed any danger coming from Dad. We both made it through the night. The next day I encouraged Dad to set up his required appointment with the local drug rehabilitation center. He said he would. I told Dad I loved him…I was praying for him. That was all the *Jesus-talk* I had in me for Dad right then…and all the *Jesus-talk* that, I figured, Dad could probably have handled from me at that moment in time.

I made it all the way back to Fairport, NY without any tears…or any policemen needing to check on me. Just a whole lot of deep cleansing-out, calming breaths. And the fleeting-escapist thoughts of just wanting to run away from this call on my life that was so demanding and bizarre. God just gave me a rub on my head – an intimate, loving, yet stern, hard little rub to my head – as a reminder of God's own demanding and bizarre call He had placed on His Son Jesus Christ...for me.

More deep breaths...only this time I was also breathing *in* the love and the grace and the truth of God by which He had set me free...and I was breathing *out* my *Thankfuls* to God for His love and presence, perspective and power in my life.

Before the third woman, after Mom's death, entered into Dad's life, Dad went to Mississippi alone in late 1995. To spend some time with his southern family. He went to stay with his Mother, who Dad referred to, and usually with a snarl in his voice, by her first name, Myrtle. We kids were taught to call her Maw-Maw. But she had never really been part of our lives. Nor had Myrtle ever really been part of Dad's life. Not the way he needed. Not when he was a child. Horrendous, violent abuse, sick incest, rejection, placement in an orphanage and the shame of parental divorce when he was just a little boy (when *good* people just didn't divorce) – were all part of Dad's history and part of his story with Myrtle and his father (who had died ten years earlier). But Dad was *there*, in Mississippi, still seeking something from Myrtle. Some love, some acceptance, maybe seeking a confession or a show of sincere remorse for her wrongdoing towards him. Something. Dad was seeking something from Myrtle to ease his pain and fill his heart. And, even though Myrtle, along with Dad's Step-Father, Daddy Hill (who had died back in 1976, and was the *only* person that I ever heard Dad speak *only* good things about), had accepted Jesus as Savior at a 1952 Billy Graham Crusade in Jackson, MS, Myrtle still could *not* give Dad what he really needed.

One night while Dad was down visiting at Maw-Maw's home, I got that *Jeremiah-burning-in-my-heart-and-in-my-bones-call-from-God,* again, and I knew I was supposed to call Dad. Doggone it! I thought I was off the hook while he was in Mississippi. After all, that's part of the *Bible-Belt*, right? And Maw-Maw was a Christian now, and so were some of his other family members. Surely, God could have one of them do the *Jesus-talk* thing with Dad. Instead of me this time. *Nope.*

When I called Dad, he seemed more present on the phone (aka not drunk or doped up right then) than he often sounded. His voice was gentle and calm. He told me that Maw-Maw's health wasn't too good. He told me about the time he had spent with one of his favorite cousins, a good Christian woman. Then, God moved me...pushed me...to gently share the gospel of Jesus, very clearly and specifically, once again, with Dad. This was the first time that God had put this *Jeremiah-burning-in-my-heart-and-in-my-bones-call-from-God* on me – to tell Dad, one more time, of the salvation of Jesus – since Dad had burned me so badly with his "...*I am jus' so damn tar'd of all the Jesus talk comin' from you. It is jus' too goddamn much. You jus' gotta stop.*"

God didn't want me to stop. And God's a lot smarter and bigger than Dad. So, very gently and quietly (and shaking inside) I shared with Dad the love, forgiveness and salvation, the peace and eternal life that Jesus had for him. Again. As I closed our conversation, I asked Dad to get one of Maw-Maw's Bibles and read for himself, after we got off the phone, a passage of Scripture that I wanted to read out loud to him right now. I told Dad the chapter and verse was *Romans 10:8-10*, asking him, again, to please read it for himself later. I read the passage aloud, explaining it to Dad as I read, and then repeated the chapter and verse reference when I finished.

***But what does it [Scripture] say?***
***"The word is near you; it is in your mouth***
***and in your heart," that is, the word of faith proclaiming:***
***That if you confess with your mouth: "Jesus is Lord,"***
***and believe in your heart***
***that God raised him from the dead, you will be saved.***
***For it is with your heart that you believe and are justified,***
***and it is with your mouth that you confess and are saved.***
Romans 10:8-10

Dad listened as I read this passage. I told Dad, *"I love you so much. Dad, I really hope and pray that you will go get one of Maw-Maw's Bibles and read Romans 8:8-10 for yourself."*

Dad stopped me right then and there. *"Now, Laney, you jus' told me that the Bible passage you wuz readin' from wuz Romans 10:8-10...not Romans 8:8-10. So, girl, which is it? If I'm gonna read it fo' myself later, you gotta tell me where it is, girl!"*

My head, my heart and my spirit leapt with joy!

This was the most wonderful, fabulous mistake I ever could have made! It was through my flaw that Jesus showed me that His unfailing love was working step-by-step, little-by-little in Dad's life...*no matter* how long and hard and hurtful the journey seemed to me. Dad actually listened to me. Dad had heard the Word of God *and* wanted to know the right reference for where he could find it on his own later!

I laughed and told Dad, *"Good for you! Yep! The passage is from Romans 10:8-10. You caught me! Be blessed, Dad, by God's love for you and as you read that passage from the Bible tonight. I'm praying for you. I love you."*

*"I knows you do, girl. I love you too."*

Click. We both hung up. And my heart danced.

*Thank You, my God, for my mistake! Thank You, my God, for softening Dad's heart...even just this little bit. Thank You so, so much!*

This little mistake of mine – and Dad correcting me for it – was a huge encouragement to my head, my heart and my spirit to keep going...to keep sharing about Jesus with Dad...to keep loving on Dad with the love and tenacity that only God could possibly give me...*no matter what*...to love Dad *not* according to the pattern of this world, but to love Dad knowing that...*No matter what...God's love is with me...and continually transforms and renews my mind.*

*Yay, God!*

The third woman that came into Dad's life, after Mom died, was Dorothy. They started dating sometime in late 1996 or early 1997. In March of 1998, Dad and Dorothy were married. (Although none of us kids witnessed this wedding as we did Dad and Elli's.) And Dorothy was a surprise.

She was an unexpected, God-showing-up-in-your-life-and-in-your-face kind of surprise. Dorothy was a Christian. Dorothy was a real *get-up-early-in-the-morning-to-pray-and-read-her-Bible* kind of Christian. *God, You are so good!* I liked Dorothy! And Dad seemed to love her.

The drama of crises and craziness was far from finished in Dad's life. There were some absolutely outrageous episodes of Dad being hospitalized for several different reasons: getting drunk...taking a fall off a ladder...or off a roof...that required surgery or, at least, time in the hospital to recover from his wounds...or overdosing on his own personal pharmacy of narcotics, stimulants and depressants ...almost to the point of no return – which could have been a complete accident *or* possibly, an attempted suicide *or* another desperate act to get attention by keeping his needs front and center...and extremely exaggerated.

Dad was hurting and in deep pain emotionally, physically and spiritually. And Dad just wasn't ready to get off the roller coaster of living from crisis to crisis – or ready to stop creating the next crisis in his life by the choices he made that put him, and seemed to keep him, in harm's way. This was how Dad had lived all the time that I knew him.

But, according to Dorothy, one thing had changed significantly in the way Dad was living. Dad wasn't hurting Dorothy. He wasn't threatening her. He wasn't hitting her. The guns and knives did not come out to frighten or wound her. Dad wasn't hurting Dorothy in any physical way. *Thank You, Lord.*

Soon after they were married, Dad and Dorothy decided to make what had been Dad's winter home for the last number of years, in DeBary, Florida (just a bit north of Orlando), their permanent home. The heat of Florida's summer was easier to take than the snow and cold of Lake Ontario's winter for Dad, still a Mississippi boy at heart, and for Dorothy, who had spent most of her life in Puerto Rico. Dad sold the New York house and the beautiful, rural property along the river where I had spent so much of my little girl time running around in the woods (hiding or climbing in the trees) or down at the river's edge where I would sit on my favorite Big Rock, spending sweet time talking with and listening to my Jesus.

I had always prayed that God would raise up other believers who would surround Dad and share with him the love and truth of Jesus. (I pray *that* for all my not-yet-believer friends and family...*It takes a village*...to express the love and truth of Jesus!) God had clearly answered that prayer in Dorothy. Dad wasn't running into the arms of Jesus just then, but he was calmer, more balanced and the periods between major crises went from weeks to months. Although Dad's body was more and more crippled from his many accidents and surgeries over the years, Dad and Dorothy got out and did some fun things together. They took some day trips, went out to restaurants, visited with friends and relatives and even took a very short cruise. And when Dad wasn't strong enough or well enough to go, Dorothy still went. She became very involved with a local church in DeBary and enjoyed the senior citizens' Bible studies, fellowship group and planned excursions. Dorothy was funny, light-hearted and faithful. She had gone through many deep hardships and hurts herself over the years. But these did not define her. Her faith in Jesus did.

And so for me, there were a number of months from late 1999 to September of 2000 that I had *a bit of a breather* in my relationship with Dad. When I called, the conversations with Dad weren't deep, but they weren't painful, stilted or angry as they often had been in the pre-Dorothy time period. Dorothy would then get on the phone to tell me what they were doing, how their health was and share with me, while Dad was sitting right next to her, how best to pray for her and for him. And Dorothy and I usually prayed together, right then, before closing out our conversation. Dorothy was a simple woman. She was a good woman. And she was a child of the Most High God. And she quietly, and yet with bold gentleness, shared her faith in Jesus with Dad.

Then, Jesus took Dorothy home. She had been in the hospital for a fairly minor ailment. The evening before Dorothy died, she and Dad had spoken on the phone to make arrangements for her discharge to come home the following day. But Dorothy never woke up that following day. She had already gone home to Jesus in the wee hours of September 2, 2000.

Dorothy was free and in the full presence of her loving Lord Jesus. Dad was not.

Shock. Numbness. Disbelief. Loneliness. And a deep depression set in and swallowed up Dad. And he swallowed more booze and more pills to deal with his pain. He didn't go out much at all...after that...anymore.

Dad's outings and social contacts were pretty limited to a couple of his neighbors, some of the workers he hired to help him care for his Florida property, the bank tellers at his local branch, his repertoire of various doctors, the local pharmacists and all the staff at a family-owned diner around the corner from his house. The diner where Dad would go almost every single day to eat his one big meal of the day. And the rest of the time, Dad would *git off his feet and rest his damn crippled legs and his ole back.* And Dad would lie in his bed for incalculable hours, watching TV – mostly old movies and game shows. (Dad could have made thousands of dollars had he ever been a contestant on

Jeopardy! He always knew the answers. Dad made up, in reading voraciously, for what he hadn't learned during his limited years of formal education. Yes, that would be part of the *antinomy* of Dad. Go figure.)

Over the next several months, I called Dad, at least, once a week. Our conversations did go deep quite often. Dad was hurting. And I would quietly share the love of Jesus with him. The love that he had also seen in Dorothy's Holy Spirit-connected, Bible reading relationship with Jesus. And Dad listened...or, at least, it seemed like he did. But mostly, Dad was just so very sad. So often sick. So often tired. So often in physical pain. And, so often, not fully present mentally – the booze and the pills had worked their numbing-dumbing magic.

I went to visit Dad in Florida on my own to see with my own eyes how he was really doing. He was functioning, but not really living. Dad was depressed and dulled, though not out of control. And much of it, I believe, was caused by the whiskey and the meds – and their combination one-two punch to his head. On another visit to Florida, the four of us, Tim, Erin, Julia and I, stopped in on Dad to take him to dinner and spend an afternoon and evening with him while we were on our way to a mini-vacation at Disney World. We asked Dad if he would like to join us at Disney for a day. *"I'm jus' not up to doin' nothin', Laney. But, y'all go on an' have fun now, y'hear."* I liked that Dad was gentler. But I hated that Dad seemed so lifeless, so sad...so just existing.

In early September 2001, Dad came up to stay with us for awhile in Newtown, PA. (This was our latest nomadic settlement – our tenth home since Tim and I were married in 1980.) Finishing his visit with us, Dad actually left our home around 8:00 am on September 11 to *travel on up* to central New York and make his rounds of *visitin' fo' a spell* with My Siblings and some of his old friends – friends that he and Mom had shared. Dad didn't know anything about the evil acts of terrorism that killed so many innocent people that day while he was driving.

As I sat in numbness and shock watching the news break, planes crash, people die, buildings fall, chaos roar and evil reign – knowing that Dad was completely oblivious...Dad had no idea what was happening – I found myself thinking how unbelievable and overwhelming it is that there could possibly be so much unseen, unknown, unacknowledged evil in our world...just as had happened in my life, in my family...the same unseen, unknown, unacknowledged evil that happens every day in the lives of individuals and in the families of so many other people. How could anyone make such evil choices? How could anyone hurt innocent people? How could anyone so disregard and so utterly destroy countless numbers of precious human lives? How could anyone so disregard and utterly destroy even one precious human life?

And for a few moments, as I sat there all by myself sobbing and suffocating because of the evil I was witnessing on such a grand scale, I was a helpless little girl, all over again. I couldn't move. Evil just came in and was ripping away at my life, my peace, my hope. And it was dark. All dark. And I was so sick and so angry and so filled with pain and helplessness. I couldn't stop the evil...and I hated *all* who would bring such cruel and ugly, evil devastation into the lives of innocents – whether to numerous people at one time...or to one little child...to one man...to one woman. I hated *all* who would hatefully choose to do anything evil against anyone at any time.

*Oh God! Help me! Help this world! Heal this world! Stop this evil, God! Help us, God! Help me! Help me to love again, God! Help me to forgive again, God! Because right now I hate! Help me be strong again, God! Help us all! We need You, Jesus! We all need You so much! I need You! Help me please, God! Don't let me stay in this broken place! Don't let me stay in this dark place! Don't let me stay in this ugly, awful hate! Help me to love again, God! Oh, God! It is Your love that has made me more than a conqueror! Help me! It is Your love that has turned me around! It is Your love that has convinced me that there is NOTHING – not the world crashing in around us as evil runs rampant destroying so many lives...not the cruelty and ignorance of my father, the complacency of my mother – there is NOTHING at all in all creation that will ever be able to separate me from Your love! Help me to live in this truth...in this power...in this perspective...in this assurance ...in being convinced, once again, of Your unfailing love! God hold my head! Help me to sense Your love! Jesus, help me to love again!*

And God did. God held me – the little girl me...and the grown woman me. God held me tightly in His love. My Jesus held my head and my heart, my body and my soul...and let me cry...and let me pour out all my anguish and hate for all the evil in gut-wrenching sobs. Because Jesus hates evil too. Jesus died for the evil that happened on September 11, 2001. Jesus died for the Holocaust. Jesus died for all the evil and sin everywhere, in every generation, in every family, in every individual. Jesus died for me and for Dad and for Mom...Jesus died for everyone.

And evil will never have the last word. Never. Jesus has the last word. Jesus conquered sin and death. Jesus conquered evil and destruction. And Jesus did it all because of, and by, His love for us.

I felt as though Jesus was massaging all of me – every fiber of my physical being...every hidden part of my mind, spirit and soul. Jesus was calling me back to the truth of His love...calling me back to knowing...and being *convinced* that His love has made me more than a conqueror...being *convinced* that His love is always with me...*no matter what.*

*No matter what...God's love is with me...and continually transforms and renews my mind.*

Jesus massaged all of me...down through my innermost being – calling me back to breathe again...to trust my God...calling me back to live as His woman...calling me back to live as a vessel of His love and light – in a world gone very dark.

I took a deep breath...and rotated my head a bit, to shake off the dark...and focus on God's love and perspective and presence. Then, I called two of my neighbors – one precious Jewish woman and one precious Catholic woman, to invite them to come over to my house to pray together. They came. And on that very evil, dark day – so outrageously incongruous with the beautiful blue, sunshine-filled sky of that day – the three of us prayed together for God to heal our world. And to help us to be vessels of God's love.

And later that night, I called Dad. God had *twirled me around,* once again. God had reset my head and my heart so that I could, courageously and authentically, love again. I was, once again, more than a conqueror through God's love...and I knew that nothing – *no matter what* – could ever separate me from the love of my Lord Jesus. I was *convinced*. So, as Dad and I talked late that evening on September 11, 2001, I told Dad that I was so thankful that he made it *up home* safely...and that I'd call him again in a couple of days. I told Dad that I loved him. And I meant it.

Jesus had the last word. And His word – His convincing, transforming, renewing word – is *love*.

# 12

## *"Behold,*
## *I am making all things new."*
### *Revelation 21:5*

*Love.* The convincing – life-transforming, peace-giving, hope-renewing, twirling-me-around – *love* of God set my head and my heart, even more determinedly, to live and love in the power and in the grace and in the truth of Jesus Christ. *No matter what.*

I was to stay continually, though ever more gently, more softly, in Dad's life – in his hurting, unwell, lost, sad, limited life. And so it went for just a little more than a year...with lots of phone calls to Dad – most of them so similar in words and tone. No real news. Because Dad wasn't really living. And he really wasn't well. Dad was still mostly *takin' it easy in b'tween goin' to one doctor or 'nother for one damn thing or sum other damn thing... needin' to git' off his bad leg an' put himself to restin' up his ole back an' his creaky, ole ar-ther-it-is filled bones.*

Dad's usual poor health was about to take an even deeper nose dive – or rather a very bad fall – that God, in His love and mercy, would use to take hold of Dad.

Mid October 2002, I got a call from Dad. *That* in itself was unusual as I was almost always the one who called him. Dad called me from his hospital room in Sanford, Florida.

*"Laney, I'm in the hospital here in Sanford. I went an' broke my goddamn hip. I was workin' up on the ladder, fixin' a light an', damn, if my bad leg didn't jus' let go out from under me. It started shakin' an' it jus' couldn't hold me no mo'. I tried like all hell to catch myself. But I jus' couldn't do it. An' I went down hard! I heard a pow'rful crack. An' felt a turr'ble, sharp pain. An' let me tell you, I done let out one helluva scream. I crawled, more like pulled myself, over to the phone. Ambulance had to come git me. Got in the 'mergency room an' the doctors had to do some surgery on my hip an' some pinnin' me back together. Right then. An' right now, I needs to stay in the hospital fo' a few mo' days. 'Cuz the doctors said that I needs to have sumbody come down here to take me home befo' they'll go ahead an' release me. So, Laney, why don't you jus' git yourself on down here an' help me out fo' a while?"*

Deep breath. *Hold my head, God. Lead my life, God. In Your Love, God. Aaaaggghhh!* Deep breath.

*"Dad, I'm so sorry this happened to you.* (Not surprised, but sorry.) *Wow. I'm so thankful you were able to get into the hospital and get your hip operated on right away. I will come down and help out, Dad. I'll come just as soon as I can. I just need to talk with Tim, first, and check out the plane schedules. It'll take me just a little bit to reorganize my schedule* (my whole life!) *and make arrangements for Julia to be sure she's all set without me."* (Erin was already a freshman at New York University in Manhattan – so she was all set without me. But Julia was a junior in high school, and was still a couple of months shy of having her

driver's license so that she could get herself back and forth to all her school, and outside school, activities.)

I was down in Florida before the end of the second day, and drove right to the hospital from the airport. Dad would be in the hospital for a couple days more before the doctors would *go ahead an' release him.* With the hospital social worker, Dad and I made plans for the visiting nurses and home-rehab staff to come to Dad's house for his follow-up care over the next several weeks. I planned to stay in Florida for the first two weeks after Dad was discharged. After that, we figured that Dad should be strong enough to manage on his own – as long as he was still receiving his in-home medical support *and* the dinners that I would arrange to be delivered to him. (Thanks to Meals-on-Wheels!)

During those *couple days more* before Dad was released, I stayed at his house. I wanted to get it cleaned up for Dad before I brought him home. *Nice thought. Shouldn't be too bad.* What I thought of as the best way to use my time *and* help Dad out in practical ways, God used as an intense period of time to help prepare my heart, and bend my knees, to be a servant and *only* a servant to my Dad.

And God had all the props ready to accomplish such a task...to accomplish His purpose.

Dad's house was absolutely gross. Not messy, really. Dad's belongings all had their places where they belonged. But the house itself was absolutely gross. Call-the-health-department-kind-of-gross. The linoleum floors throughout the kitchen and hallway were completely covered with multiple layers of rubbed-in crud and grease. The carpets were stained from food and drink spills and streaked with outside dirt and mud that had found its way inside. Everything – cupboards, tables, countertops, fridge, stove, microwave, coffee maker, dishes, doors, windows, knick-knacks and the shelves they were sitting on – had a sticky, thick, grimy film over them where filth, Florida dust and humidity had mixed together with the cigarette smoke from Dad's chain-smoking habit. (Which was also evident in the tell-tale burn marks on almost every imaginable surface in Dad's house.) The smoke had not only mixed with the dirt and humidity to *cover* everything, the smoke had also *soaked* its way into every fabric and material in the house – easy chairs, cushions, sofas, beds, pillows, sheets, blankets, towels, every box of food, every magazine, every newspaper, every book, every piece of note paper and even into the toilet paper. *Gross.*

And then there were the little lizards, big spiders and, my personal favorite, the cockroaches.

*God, You are so demanding. God, You are so good.*

God knew that I needed to be physically, mentally and spiritually down on my hands and knees – scrubbing off the filth...or stretching up into ceiling corners and to the back shelves to wipe away webs, dead bugs and soaked-in dirt... or reaching down into oh-my-goodness-such-disgusting toilets – in order to be able to best love and serve Dad. I needed to be right in the middle of the physical filth...and still keep on moving, keep on cleaning, keep on praying, keep on singing and keep on loving...*no matter what.*

I was worn out and grossed out. But God's love – God's humbling and humorous love – kept me going in spite of the yuck. Being so physically tired from this *hard labor of love* actually helped to quiet my spirit so that I could listen more fully...more completely uncovered and vulnerably to my God.

The second day after I had gotten Dad home from the hospital, and settled him back into his room after making him some lunch, I decided it was time to attack his living room knick-knacks – one-by-one – as my next feat of purification. (For them and for me!) The BIG jobs were done. It was time to take on the tedious-time-consuming-make-me-crazy-in-the-details-cleaning-jobs. It was time to clean all of the nooks and crannies that belonged to all of the strange collectibles that were filling Dad's shelves. Clocks, model cars, a rose-in-a-glass-ball, a pretty little deer, decorative baskets and candy dishes made from milk-glass or blown glass, several figurines and statues – some made of fine china, some made of ceramic, wood or hard plastic. Most of these knick-knacks I recognized from my childhood home. A few were probably Dorothy's additions. There was no theme to the knick-knacks. It was all just stuff. Stuff that had been collected. Stuff that had now collected – and was coated by – that sticky, thick, grimy film made from the mixing of filth, Florida dust, humidity and cigarette smoke.

To clean these, I had to stand on the same ladder from which Dad had fallen. I had barely gotten myself into a perfectly balanced, ready-to-clean position, when I picked up the first collectible. And started to cry. Really cry. It was a tears-streaming-down-my-face, sobs-rising-from-my-gut, snot-dripping-from-my-nose-to-my-chin kind of cry.

I wasn't expecting this. My plan was to quietly and meditatively pray for Dad as I cleaned all those collectibles he had collected. Instead, an overwhelming, unanticipated flood of sadness and agony was washing over me and coming from within me. But it wasn't for me. It was for Dad. It wasn't all from me. It was from God too. I felt as if the Spirit of God was crying, *in utterances too deep for words*...crying for Dad...crying through me...crying with me. My heart was absolutely broken for Dad. And my heart was broken for God. I sensed, on a level that I had never sensed before, the aching, longing love of our God who wants no one to be lost...no one to reject His love and condemn themselves. God wanted – God had always wanted – Dad to turn to Him...to know His love and to be held by His love forever.

And God's Spirit and I – as the Spirit was pushing me and flooding through all of me...through all of my mind, body and spirit – were crying for Dad's pain. Crying for all of the pain within Dad's mind, body and spirit. Crying for all of the pain he had caused others. Crying for all of Dad's shame and guilt. Crying for all of the shame and guilt he had caused others. Crying for Dad's blindness. Crying for Dad's selfishness. Crying for Dad's stubbornness. Crying for Dad's brokenness.

God's Spirit and I were crying – passionately and pitifully – for Dad's lost life.

And we were begging for Dad's life. Fighting for Dad's life. God's Spirit and I were crying out...crying out God's own deepest desires *back* to our God – back to our Almighty God...back to our Lord Jesus, the Only Savior... back to our own, true Abba – to rescue and to save Dad's life. To reach him and hold him by our God's unfailing, passionate love. Now and for all eternity.

Standing on that ladder, tenuously balanced, tenaciously cleaning every nook and cranny of those scummy collectibles – God gave me a small, though astounding, sense of how overwhelming and powerful His passion and love truly are for His lost and sin-marred people. Every collectible needed to be picked up, carefully handled and completely cleaned. The world-assigned value, based on the outward appearance and the type of material that made up each of these collectibles – from the finest of china to the cheapest of plastic – didn't matter. Every collectible was worth this time. Every collectible was worth this effort. The china, glass and ceramic collectibles had chips and jagged edges. The wood and plastic collectibles had deep, wound-like scratches and dirt stubbornly stuck in their grooves and gouged-out places. Almost all the collectibles had pieces and parts that were missing. None were perfect. Not anymore. Not now. Maybe not ever. Yet, every collectible was to be lifted up with tenderness and respect. Every collectible was to be washed off, scrubbed perfectly clean and set back down...and stood back up...in its renewed and transformed state.

And God's Spirit and I were crying out to our Holy, Intimate and Sovereign God to do exactly the same for Dad.

Dad only wanted a little bit of supper that night. He was tired and in pain. He was *"jus' gonna eat"* what I brought to him in his room. *"Laney, I'm jus' fixin' to watch me sum ole movies 'till I'm so rum-dumb that I jus' fall to sleep. Don' feel much like gittin' up outta this bed right now."*

I got Dad all settled with his supper, cleaned it up after and made sure Dad was as calm and comfortable for the evening as I possibly could. Then, I took a drive. And I took myself out for what would become my own *Therapy Meal* at the Cheesecake Factory in Winter Park, Florida – avocado eggrolls with a tamarind-cashew dipping sauce, a glass of dry red wine, a piece of their Godiva Chocolate Cheesecake and a cup or two of coffee.

I lingered over my meal. I sent up my thankful prayers to my kind and generous God for this beautiful respite of time and this soul-feeding meal. I was *present in the moment*...right there, just there. No place else. No one else. Just God with me. I sat there, worn out from the intensity of that afternoon, but peaceful and thankful. And very quiet. I was just slowly eating, tasting and enjoying every single bite, sip, flavor, texture and aroma that my *Therapy Meal* offered me. (And probably making *yummy noises* as I did. As I've been told I make.) All of the Cheesecake Factory staff members were gracious and warm, allowing me to sit there for hours. (Having, and reading from, my open Bible at the table might have helped the staff understand my need to keep the table and their need to just let me be. It's the old *I-got-my-Bible-so-back-away-from-me-strategy*.)

I took deep breaths. Lots of them. I thanked God for quieting my soul, one level at a time, and for strengthening my head and heart to new depths with His love...with His amazing, crying out, tender and unfailing love that holds me. And wants to hold Dad. *No matter what.*

I slept well that night. Even with the little lizards, big spiders and cockroaches that were still present in spite of my best cleaning efforts. With my own (clean) sweatshirt over my pillow to help block some of its smoke-soaked smell, I snuggled down into my bed and into my Abba's arms to rest from the hard work – the hard physical, emotional and spiritual work – of that day. And I slept well. I trusted my Abba. He loved me. He loved Dad.

Sleeping well at Dad's house wasn't the easiest thing to do. I was often sleep-deprived when staying with Dad. And not just because of the little lizards, big spiders and cockroaches that I knew were ever-present and scurrying all around me. I often couldn't sleep well because of the monsters – physical, mental, emotional and spiritual monsters – that would cause Dad to scream out in the night. Loud, harsh, angry, helpless, hurting, semi-unconscious screams would come from Dad. Two to several times in the night. Dad would scream out in physical pain caused from the throbbing, searing agony in his wounded hip, or his crippled back or his bad leg. The pills just didn't seem to hold the physical pain during the night. And Dad would scream out in emotional and mental pain – probably coming from the throbbing, searing agony of unhealed wounds that Dad himself had suffered. Or maybe some of Dad's night-terror, monster-induced screams came from the throbbing, searing agony of knowing the anguish he had caused someone else. Agony that Dad could ignore during the day but replayed in the night and caused him to scream out as he tried to fight away the monsters.

The next morning, I brought Dad in his coffee. He said he slept *purdy good* too. *"I only had to git up onst in the night 'cuz I wuz hurtin' so bad an' had to git myself to the toilet. Glad those nurses done brought in that high seater commode fo' me. I don' know what I'd do without that."*

I was glad, too, for that *high seater commode*. And thankful that Dad was able *to git himself to the toilet* and back to bed without falling...and that, somehow, I had slept through it.

By late morning, Dad was ready for a real meal. And ready to eat out at the kitchen table, although he stayed seated in his wheelchair. We just chatted lightly while we ate. Talking about some of his neighbors. Dad went on for awhile about *"...what a big help Claude is to me. He's a gooood man. Keeps my lawn mowed fo' me. Checks up on me jus' 'bout ever' day. But oh Lord-y! Claude does like to talk! A lot. But that's okay. 'Cuz whenever it gits to be too much fo' me 'cuz I git to hurtin' real bad, I jus' tell Claude to git himself on over home. An' he does. Claude is one gooood man. He knows when I needs him jus' to leave me be. An' he still keeps comin' round to check up on me. He'd either come on over to visit me in the hospital or he'd call me up on the telephone nearly ever' day b'fo' you got yourself on down here."*

Claude and I had already spent a lot of time talking, both outside Dad's house and inside Dad's house. One morning Claude stood over by the kitchen door while I scrubbed off two or three of the scummy, grimy layers from the kitchen floor. He really was *a gooood man.* And I thanked God for Claude's kindness to Dad. And for Dad's kindness to him. Dad had pretty much given Claude one of his cars to use whenever he needed it. And if they ever went out to eat together, it was pretty much always Dad who paid for their meals. Those little ways of helping people are not only right for us to do, but they're good for our souls. And it was good for Dad to be thought of as generous and willing to help others out in the ways that he could help. And he really did. This was part of the *antinomy* of Dad. Claude *only* knew Dad here in DeBary, Florida. He didn't know Dad's history. Dad could just be who he was, right then, as Claude's neighbor. To Claude, Dad was a man with some serious health problems and whose sweet wife (of only two years), Dorothy, had died two years ago. Claude knew that Dad could be generous and get angry. Dad appreciated Claude – and Claude knew that too. And he was happy to help Dad out.

Dad and I finished eating. I got us two more hot cups of coffee and sat back down facing Dad. And then it came. It came gently, but it came unmistakably. Once again, the *Jeremiah-burning-in-my-heart-and-in-my-bones-call-from-God* came on me. And I was to tell Dad, one...more...time, of the salvation of Jesus Christ. (And inside my head I was more deeply aware – because of the crying-out time with God's Spirit just the afternoon before – that this renewed *Jeremiah-burning-in-my-heart-and-in-my-bones-call-from-God* was coming from the very heart of our Almighty God who loves Dad with an indescribable passion and pursues him persistently and purposefully. Because God wanted to save Dad's life – now and for all eternity.)

Before I spoke with Dad, I had a conversation with God.

*"Just jump in, Sylane. I'm here. I love you. I love your Dad."*

*"Okay, God. I know. I love You too. My stomach's pretty sick, God."*

*"I know. Jump in now. It's okay. I'm here. I love you. I love your Dad."*

Very quietly and very gently, I spoke with Dad. No physical strength was left in me. God had taken it from me by keeping me on my hands and knees for most of the last few days. Very lovingly, very humbly and with an intense depth of passion that came from God, I spoke with Dad.

*"Dad, I love you so much...*long pause...*I care so much about your healing for your hip and your strength for your body. And I want to do whatever I can to help you get better. But I don't have the power to make you all better."*

*"I know, Laney. But, I'm glad you got yourself down here to do what you can for this ole man."*

*"Dad, I care about your soul even more. You know I love you. You've heard me tell you about the love and forgiveness and salvation of Jesus so many times. Dad, I just have to ask you: Who is Jesus to you?"*

*"Well, Laney, your two brothers have been talkin' to me 'bout Jesus a lot lately too. They wants to know if I'm gonna let Jesus be my Savior."* (Thank you, My Big Brother and My Little Brother, for *talkin'* to Dad about Jesus too! We are all part of the Body of Christ and we need each other! ...*and it takes a village...*)

*"Dad, I want to know. Are you ready to let Jesus be your Savior? Are you ready to let God hold you in His love, hold you in His forgiveness and hold you there for all eternity?"*

*"Well, Laney..."*

Dad went on for a bit, *talkin'* quietly, but not answering the question. He couldn't really look at me. Dad was moving his hands on top of the table – with his finger tips doing a kind of dance on the table's surface. He *wuz talkin' 'bout* other family members who had accepted Jesus as their Savior – Aunt Betty, his sister...Uncle H.C., his brother...Mom before she died...Dorothy...one of Dad's nephews...even Myrtle...and his step-daddy, Daddy Lee. *"Yep. They all believed in Jesus as their Savior. They all let God hold them."*

My heart was aching so badly for Dad. I wanted so much for him. God wanted even more.

*"Dad, please, please stop dancing around this. I love you so much. I want you to let God hold you. I want you to let Jesus come in to be your Savior."*

*"Laney, I'm not dancin' 'round this."* Dad was still so calm, so quiet. Not agitated at all. He had no strength left in him either.

*"Laney, I'll tell ya, when I wuz 'bout eighteen years old, I did know that Jesus wuz the Savior. I did. But, I did not let Him hold me then."*

Dad looked so sad. So tired. Dad's moving hands and dancing fingers, with the now long, *gray* (instead of *black*) hair on them, just stopped. Dad rested his hands on the tabletop, palms down, making his missing trigger-finger on his right hand seem even more obviously absent than ever.

*"Dad, God is ready to hold you now."* Dad lifted his head and looked right at me as I continued speaking. *"You just need to believe what Jesus has already done for you. He died for you, Dad. He died for me. He died to forgive us and give us the salvation and the eternal life that only comes through Him. We both need Jesus, Dad. God wants to hold you so much. He loves you so much, Dad. Are you ready to let God hold you now?"*

Dad pushed back just a little bit away from the kitchen table and rested his elbows on his wheelchair's arm pads. Dad folded his hands together in front of his chest. *Those hands* – that were so very scarred up from the ravages of so many more years of cutting and banging and hitting and falling...*those hands* that were gnarled and twisted with *ar-ther-it-is* and deeply yellowed at his nails from years of *smokin'* and *drinkin'*...*those hands* that had caused me and My Mom and My Big Sister and My Oldest Brother and My Big Brother and My Little Brother so very much pain... so very much shame...so very much fear...*those hands* that had ripped and torn away from me all of my little girl innocence and all of my twirling around joy – *those hands* were now quietly folded together in front of Dad's chest.

*"Yes, Laney. I'm ready to let God hold me now."*

I dropped to one knee in front of Dad. And I put my hands over his hands that were still folded together in front of his chest, and we prayed. And Dad let Jesus hold him as his Savior.

I was overwhelmed with thankfulness...washed with a deep and quiet and indomitable thankfulness...that took my breath away...and gave it back again. God had rescued and saved my Dad, right then and there. The evil, ugly, sin-wielding, destructive powers of hell had been broken off from Dad and completely crushed as Dad *let Jesus hold him*, right then and there, as Dad sat in his wheelchair with his hands folded in front of his chest.

Still holding those hands of Dad's, and with a few tears falling down my face, I kissed Dad's face. And I whispered in his ear, *"Dad, I love you. And, now, I know that God has answered my prayer so that we will never be eternally separated."*

Dad remembered the letter that I had written almost thirty years earlier. *"No, Laney, we won't be eternally separated. An', Laney, I wants you to know, if only I had let God hold me when I wuz a younger man, I never would'uv done the things to y'all that I done."*

*Oh-my-goodness. Oh, my Holy Lord.* I wasn't looking for that. I had already forgiven Dad years ago. But the Spirit of God had convicted Dad of his sins, moved Dad to this confession and freed Dad from the condemnation he deserved because of his sins...all at the same time.

Our God's love is merciful, powerful and transforming beyond my comprehension. And I am *convinced* that God's love changes everything. And makes everything new.

I looked into Dad's eyes, and God gave me a sweet and precious gift – a gift of assurance and love from the very heart of God. As I looked into my Dad's eyes, they changed. Dad's eyes changed *from* the blood-shot, yellow-tinged, angry, evil, self-pitying, cold, hard, steely-blue eyes that I had seen almost every time I had looked into them... *to* the clearest, most beautiful of bright, light blue eyes, shining with the innocence...and filled with the love that Jesus had just poured into Dad. And for a few moments, Jesus let me see this tangible, physical evidence – in my Dad's now beautiful, baby-blue eyes – of the purifying, transforming work that Jesus had done in my Dad's soul...for all eternity.

And I sensed my Sovereign God, my Holy Lord Jesus, saying:

### *Behold, I am making all things new...*
Revelation 21:5

As I stood back on my feet, I gave Dad another kiss on his face and squeezed his still folded hands, one more time, and said, *"Happy Birthday, Dad. Happy Birthday and Welcome Home."*

I sat back down in my kitchen chair, just a few feet from Dad. We just sat there, very thankful, for a few moments... and we both went quietly into our own heads and thoughts. Dad broke the silence, speaking gently, but almost with a bit of pleading in his voice...and on a subject I was not expecting.

*"Laney, I knows I've done a lot of awful things in my life. But I needs you to know that I did not drown those*

*little kittens. I knows you an' the other kids always thought I did. But I did not drown them. They must'uv jus' fallen in that water. I did not hurt them. An' I needs you to believe me."*

I was immediately spun back to being a little girl, squatting down just outside the back door to our addition that had been built onto the trailer. I was in my little red short-sleeved sweater and my little green shorts. No shoes. My hair was short, so it was after Dad had cut all my long, beautiful hair off. I was looking down just under the flat, little wooden bridge walkway that Dad had put in place from the back door to level ground. Underneath this little bridge was a small trench where rain water always gathered after a rainstorm. And just the night before, we had one really big storm. I looked down into the muddy pool below me...and there they were...four or five beautiful, little yellow kittens all wet and dirty. All dead. I was crying so hard as I reached down and picked one of those little, yellow kittens up. I was so sad. And I was so angry. I knew that Dad didn't like that stray Mama-Cat that had come around lately. I knew Dad didn't want any of her kittens around either. And as I held that one little, yellow kitten and was reaching down to take another one out of its drowning pool, Dad came up behind me. He had been in one of the backyard tool-sheds working.

*"Laney, what'cha got there."*

I couldn't talk. I just looked at Dad. He killed dogs. He hurt us. I just looked at him and wondered how he could kill...how he could drown these fluffy, little, innocent, yellow kittens. But I didn't say a word. I just looked at him. And I hated him.

I put the little yellow kittens down as gently as I possibly could. I just stared at Dad in my silent accusation ...in my sadness and anger. And then I ran from him. I ran from that big, bad, kitten-killing man.

As I ran down to the river, I heard Dad call out to me. *"Laney, git back here. I didn't hurt these here kittens. Laney, I did not do this."*

I didn't come back. And I didn't believe him.

But now, here was Dad, at seventy-three years of age, asking me...gently pleading with me, at my forty-two years of age, to believe him. Believe that this one ugly and cruel thing – for which I had falsely accused him through the look in my eyes and the running of my feet – he had *not* done. Dad needed me to believe him fully *and* to help set him fully free from all accusations – *whether* those accusations were grounded in truth because of what Dad had done *or* those accusations were wrongfully made because of other things Dad had done.

It was time for freedom.

I reached over to take Dad's right hand that was now resting on his knee. *"Dad, I'm so sorry that I blamed you for drowning those little kittens. I'm so sorry that I hurt you. Forgive me. I believe you, Dad."*

*"I jus' needed you to know the truth 'bout them kittens, Laney."*

*"Thank you, Dad. Thank you for telling me. Let's both let God hold us really tightly now."*

And we squeezed hands and took another sip of our, now, not-so-hot coffees. Dad and I were at peace with our God and with each other. We were quiet. We were full. We were freer than either of us had ever been. And we both sighed big sighs. God had done a mighty, eternally-transforming work of love that day for the soul of my Dad...and for the joy of our Lord.

I helped Dad *git back to bed and rest up a bit b'fo' the visitin' nurse wuz to come on over* to check his surgical wound that was left open to help it drain better.

God was now holding Dad. Holding him for all eternity. God had cleaned all the poison from Dad's spirit by the holy blood of Jesus. *And nothing in all creation would be able to separate Dad from the love of God that is in Christ Jesus our Lord.* And nothing in all eternity would be able to separate Dad from me. We were spending it together with Jesus.

And I was humbled and awed and filled with the Spirit's passionate love song for my God. My heart soared and spirit sang *in utterances too deep for words*...while my mind kept repeating...*Thank You. Thank You. Thank You, my Lord, my King, my Abba, my Jesus. I love You. I love You. I love You.*

On that day, October 18, 2002, Dad's life was eternally changed. On that day Dad was eternally made new.

Sadly, Dad still had to face many days of unimaginable pain, sickness, infections, numerous surgeries, hospitalizations and rehab unit stays over the next four years...until Jesus would finally call him home on July 12, 2006.

And over those next four years, I built up a whole lot of frequent flier miles. On my second trip down to help Dad out, I was joined by My Big Sister. Dad was now being treated by specialists and surgeons in the Orlando Regional Medical Center, so My Big Sister and I planned to stay at a local hotel instead of trekking back and forth to DeBary. When the surgical waiting room nurse heard we weren't from Florida, she made arrangements for us to stay at the beautiful and affordable (and completely cockroach free!) *Hubbard House* – a warm and loving place to stay with delicious meals for patients and families from out-of-town. *Wow! Thank You, Lord!* Hubbard House became my home away from home over those next four years, and a place where My Big Brother also joined me during another one of Dad's medical crises. Over those next four years, I spent a whole lot of time in doctors' offices, hospitals and rehab units. I spent a whole lot of time talking with physicians, surgeons, nurses, orderlies, physical therapists, medical social workers *and* Claude. And I ate a whole lot of my favorite *Therapy Meals* at the Cheesecake Factory in Winter Park.

Dad went through so much over those four years. He was so often sick. So often in pain. So often in surgery or trying to recover from surgery. Almost all of Dad's life was now limited to dealing with the breakdown of his physical body. There weren't a whole lot of opportunities for Dad to be ministered to or to be encouraged in his new relationship with Jesus. Dad was barely hanging on in so many ways.

In spite of it all, in October 2004, Dad was doing a little bit better or, at least, he was going for a longer stretch of time in between hospital stays. During one of our usual phone calls I had made to Dad in early October, Dad told me, *"Laney, I think I'm gonna plan me another trip to come on up your way to see y'all, an' then I'll go on up to New York after that to see the rest of the fam'ly."*

*"Great, just let me know when you plan on coming, Dad. You know you're always welcomed."*

A few days later in the early evening, I got one of those rare phone calls that were initiated by Dad. *"Laney, I got me all the way up here to Newtown, Penn-syl-van-i-a on*

*Route 95. I am plumb tar'd out an' I'm jus' sittin' here at the Rite Aid. Now, I don' know how to git to your house from here. So, you know what I'm gonna let you do fo' me?"*

(Every time I think of Dad using that line – and he used it more than usual during those particular four years of his life, *"You know what I'm gonna let you do for me?"* – I just want to burst out laughing and say, *"No, Dad! What are you gonna let me do for you? I can hardly wait to find out!"* Because that line would inevitably be followed by a request for something Dad was *gonna let me do for him* like *cuttin' his big, ole, thick, ugly, yellowed toenails...*or *cleanin' up the bathroom he had just messed in...or... makin' up his bed with fresh sheets 'cuz his wound was oozin' out all over tar-nation agin...or...runnin' on out to the pharmacy...or...drivin' on over to his fav'rit burger place to pick him up an extra large chocolate milkshake cuz' that sounded real good to him jus' then...or...*)

So, there was Dad, having driven straight for just about one thousand miles from DeBary, Florida to Newtown, Pennsylvania since early that morning. And he was *plumb tar'd out an' jus' sittin' at the Rite Aid.*

*"Laney, you know what I'm gonna let you do for me? I'm gonna let you drive on over here an' git me so I can follow you home. 'Cuz I jus' can't git there by myself."*

*Oh, my goodness!* My relationship with Dad was no longer brutal...but it definitely was not predictable...or easy! *Hold my head, God! Let me love, God!*

*"Okay, Dad! Tim's home so we'll both come over and get you right now."*

And we did. Dad stayed in bed most of the next two days trying to recover. He was absolutely exhausted –

physically and mentally. This would have been an incredible feat, though still every bit as crazy, if someone fully healthy and a whole lot younger than my seventy-five year old Dad had driven straight through for those one thousand miles...all in one day...all alone. That was Dad. Got something in his head...or had something to prove...and he was darn sure going to do it.

Since the time that Dad *had let God hold him,* he had not been able to go to church. Mostly because of his multiple medical problems and all the time he spent in hospitals and rehab facilities. And I think, too, that Dad probably didn't really want to go to church *all by himself* in Florida, even if he did feel physically strong enough to go on a particular Sunday. But by Sunday, October 10, 2006, Dad had recovered well enough from his ego-driven-road-trip to come to the worship service with us at our home church, Grace Point, in Newtown, PA. Like so many other protestant churches, Grace Point regularly offers their Communion Service on the first Sunday of every month. But *not* this month. *Not* this October. This month, because of glitches in the schedule and visiting missionaries – *and because God wanted Dad to be there with me* – Grace Point offered their Communion Service on the second Sunday of the month, on October 10.

And there we sat side by side, as the Bread and the Cup were passed, first, to Dad...he then passed them to me...and I passed them on to my Tim. And together, as Dad and Daughter, as Brother and Sister in Christ, we took Communion together for the first time in our lives. Dad and I joined together *in remembrance of Jesus*...and we gave thanks for His body that was broken, that was sacrificed for us...and we gave thanks for His blood that was poured out for the forgiveness of our sins. We were loved by our God. And it had changed everything and made everything new.

We were asked to stand and sing a song at the close of Communion. Dad used his crutch under his right arm to help maneuver himself to a standing position. He rested his left hand on the seat in front of him. I rested both my hands on the seat in front of me, to help keep me steady. The tears had started to flow slowly down my face. I was overwhelmed by the transforming grace of Jesus. I was humbled and thankful and in absolute awe of how God's love changes everything.

The song that we were asked to stand up and sing was, "I Believe in Jesus."[2] And there we were. Dad and I were standing and making a profession of faith in our Lord Jesus Christ – and we were making it together as we sang:

*I believe in Jesus*
*I believe He is the Son of God*
*I believe He died and rose again*
*I believe He paid for us all*

*And I believe He is here now*
*Standing in our midst*
*Here with the power to heal now*
*And the grace to forgive*

*I believe in You, Lord*
*I believe You are the Son of God*
*I believe You died and rose again*
*I believe You paid for us all*

*And I believe You're here now*
*Standing in our midst*
*Here with the power to heal now*
*And the grace to forgive*

The first time that we sang the second stanza in the chorus, *"Here with the power to heal now...and the grace to forgive,"* I was moved to the very core of my being, once again, by the reality...by the freeing truth – that it was only by the powerful love of my God that He poured into me, as I became a *bucket* – that I could ever have been healed so completely from such horrendous, evil and ugly abuse. And it was only by the unlimited love of my God, that I could ever have become a *bucket* to then pour out and offer the beautiful, life-renewing grace of Jesus Christ to my Dad.

And with tears still flowing down my cheeks, but keeping myself from sobbing too hard, I reached out my hand to take hold of Dad's hand that was resting on the seat in front of him. And with all my heart I held Dad's hand and sang those words. *"Here with the power to heal now ...and the grace to forgive."*

And there we were. Dad and I standing together with *Jesus standing in our midst.* I was crying and I wanted to give Dad respect and space, so I gently slipped my hand to rest it back on the seat in front of me. Then that line from the chorus came again. *"Here with the power to heal now ...and the grace to forgive."*

And this time, it was Dad who reached out his old and gnarled, once-pain-and-shame-inflicting hand to take hold of my hand. Dad's hand, with its long, gray hair was now reaching out to take hold of my hand as a *Daddy* should. And Dad could do this now because he was being held in the perfect hands of his Abba, his Father God.

God does not change. But God's love radically changed me...and Dad.

*Thank You, my Jesus. Thank You.*

# After Thoughts

## *"He who has ears, let him hear..."*
### *Matthew 11:15*

Early morning on July 12, 2006, I got a call from Dad's friend and neighbor Claude.

*"Sylane, I am so sorry to tell you this, sweetheart, but your Dad is dead. There was a fire in his house. There's all sorts of policemen and firemen and investigators over at his house to find out what exactly happened. Sweetheart, I'm so sorry to have to tell you about your Dad. But I'm so glad I had your number in my mobile phone. I don't know how long it will be before they know exactly how your Dad died."*

It really doesn't matter. Dad was dead. Dead to this earth forever. But because Dad had finally *let God hold him*, Dad was now welcomed into the eternal, unfailing, inseparable embrace of the love of his Lord Jesus Christ.

I am *convinced* of it.

And I am *convinced* that our Mighty God, our Savior Jesus Christ, wants you to be held by His unfailing, inseparable, eternal embrace of love. Jesus poured out His life on the cross for the forgiveness of our sins. And Jesus conquered the power of sin and death through His resurrection.

*He who has ears, let him hear*...and *believe*...and *live* in the saving grace of our Lord Jesus Christ.

And I am *convinced* that God's eternal, unfailing, inseparable love is more than able to heal, transform and break off every chain and every bondage of all your pain and shame so that you, too, may live in the power of the grace, truth and freedom of our Lord Jesus Christ.

*He who has ears, let him hear*...and *believe*...and *receive* this passionately transforming, twirling-you-around love from our Mighty God that changes everything. Our hearts. Our heads. Our perspectives. Our lives.

Jesus did this for me. And God doesn't change. He can do the same for you. Of this, I am *Convinced!*

# *Thankfuls*

My *Thankfuls,* first, go to my Abba, my Jesus and God's omnipresent, outrageously intimate Spirit. Because of You I am alive. By Your love I am transformed. I am Yours. My life is Yours. I am Your audience. I love You, God.

And I lift up my *Thankfuls* for *the three* who God so lovingly put in my life to share it with in the most beautiful of ways. *My Tim*, I can hardly say your name before tears of deep thankfulness and flowing joy begin to dance down my face. You are the best. God uses you to bring out His best in me. I love you, *My Timmy,* with all that I am...you are mine and I am yours. *My Erin and My Julia*, my babies, my beautiful women, my sisters, my friends – you both have taught me so much about God's heart, about His uncompromising love and His crazy, passionate joy. I want to be like you when I grow up! I love you both forever and ever...*and maybe even longer!*

My *Thankfuls* go out for *My Editorial Team,* three faithful, truth-telling and *very different* people who have given me their love, wisdom and generosity of time to walk this very intimate of walks with me. Praying with me. Crying with me. Rejoicing with me...in awe of God's love story to all of us! For *Robyn McCloskey*, aka Chucky (think doll and dagger!) who, on February 27, 2009, God used to get me to *His* starting point for *Convinced!* – a very ugly and evil place in order to show the absolute beauty and power of our Lord Jesus Christ's healing and transforming love; for *Dave Ridder,* my wise, challenging, encouraging, strengthening, beautiful, pastoral guide, whose words, *"Don't Compromise,"* resonate with my soul as coming from the very heart and mind of the Living God; and for *DeAnne Harland,* my *constant* prayer partner, ministry partner, encourager, friend and hard-working, detailed-focused script editor, who has walked this walk with me more intimately than anyone else and with whom I can take a deep breath. I love and thank all three of you with all my heart!

My *Thankfuls* to God, who works in the details, go up for Julie Power – my eleventh hour script editor!

And for *My Cover Design Team,* two gifted and giving children of God, my *Thankfuls* sing out! For *Curtis Peters,* my brother-son-friend in faith and cover designer (and website designer!), who opened himself fully to the Spirit's power and voice to design and cover *Convinced!* with God's transforming love; and for my younger faith-sister and cover photographer, *Janine Bergey,* who through her eyes of innocence and trust captured the heart-desires of all *Little Ones* who need God's twirling-around, healing love. I love you both so much!

I have such joy in *My Littlest of Littles,* who twirled with me at the river's edge to lift up our *Thankfuls* to Jesus for His love – and for this cover picture to be taken! My *Thankfuls* twirl and dance out, too, for your loving Daddy and Mommy and *My Other Two Littles* – your Brother and Sister. I love each one of you! And with you, I celebrate the beautiful truth that the grace of Jesus transforms us all!

My *Thankfuls* overflow for the support I have received from *My Brothers and Sisters of Transformed by Grace.* For our *TBG Board of Directors*: Lydia Austin, DeAnne Harland, Karen Secrest and Francisco Batres, Keith Brown, Andy Chirico, Tim Mack, Chris McCloskey and Dave Ridder – your love, humility, unity, sacrifice of time, energy and effort for our Lord and *TBG,* your constant encouragement to me and your vision for *Convinced!* have blessed me and shown me, ever more fully, the love of our Almighty God. For our *TBG Staff (past and present)*: Lydia Austin, Mindy Benjamin, Cathy Buser, Kristin Chace, DeAnne Harland *(Yep! She does it all!),* Rachel Mack, Carol Mehl and Teresa Warren – I am awed by the weaving of lives and spiritual gifts that our Lord continually brings to this ministry and to me personally. For our *TBG Partners in Grace* – who share their time sacrificially to surround us in deep and committed prayer and give their resources generously to help meet our practical needs as we minister to others with the love of God that sets the captives free and transforms lives – right now and for all eternity! *Darlin's,* I love you all!

*Now to him who is able to do immeasurably more than all we ask or imagine, according to his power that is at work within us, to him be glory in the church and in Christ Jesus throughout all generations, for ever and ever! Amen.*

*Ephesians 3:20-21*

Coming from a background of horrendous emotional, physical and sexual abuse, Sylane Mack is unflinchingly convinced that GOD is greater than our greatest pains, shames and fears. With passionate strength, vulnerability, wisdom and humor, Sylane shares her own life journey at conferences and retreats booked through the ministry of Transformed by Grace, Inc., for which she serves as President, Principal Speaker and Lead Counselor.

Sylane encourages and challenges her audience to consider and accept the power of the love of Jesus Christ that has radically and eternally transformed her life...the love of God that she is absolutely convinced is able to heal and renew the most broken of hearts and forgive the most evil of sins.

The love and healing that Jesus has brought into her life still humbles and holds Sylane in awe as *the audience* to God. With joy and passion Sylane recognizes that her life belongs to Jesus! She is thankful to share this life with Tim, her fabulously loving husband and very best-friend...and with her beautiful all-grown-up daughters, Erin and Julia...and with the loves of *their* lives!

Spending time with her family and good friends, being near rivers, lakes and oceans, traveling, good food, hiking, biking and Triple-Vente-Non-Fat-Cappuccinos from Starbucks make her heart sing and her feet dance!